PREPPER'S
DEHYDRATOR
HANDBOOK

LONG-TERM FOOD STORAGE TECHNIQUES
FOR NUTRITIOUS, DELICIOUS, LIFESAVING MEALS

SHELLE WELLS

Ulysses Press

Published in the United States by:
Ulysses Press
P.O. Box 3440
Berkeley, CA 94703
www.ulyssespress.com

Printed in Canada by Marquis Book Printing

ISBN: 978-1-61243-786-6
Library of Congress Control Number: 2018930843

Acquisitions editor: Casie Vogel
Managing editor: Claire Chun
Project editor: Shayna Keyles
Proofreader: Renee Rutledge
Front cover and interior design: what!design @ whatweb.com
Cover artwork: all from shutterstock.com: dried cherry tomatoes © Sergiy
    Bykhunenko; dried golden kiwis © corners74; dried sweet potatoes ©
    julie deshaies; dried meat © successo images; dried apples © marketlan
Interior artwork: page 48 © TotemArt/shutterstock.com
Production: Caety Klingman

Distributed by Publishers Group West

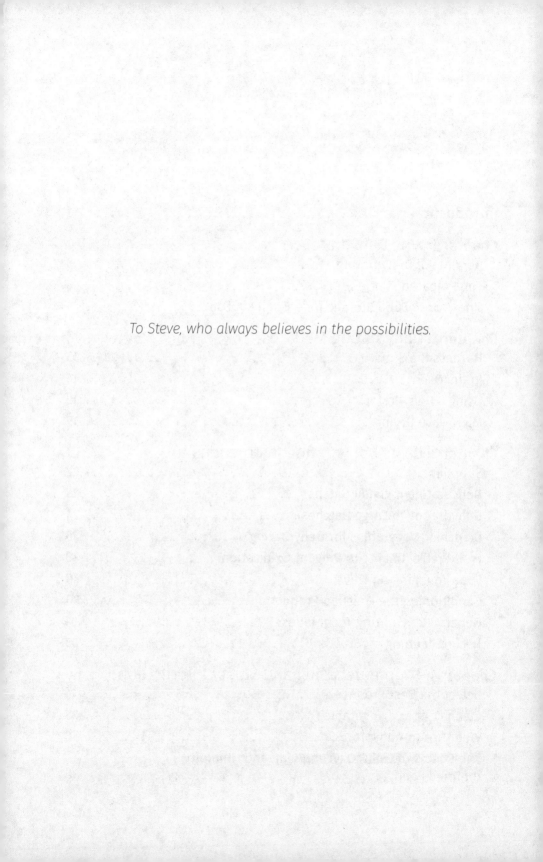

To Steve, who always believes in the possibilities.

CONTENTS

Chapter 10: Recipes 122

Pantry Basics

Snacks

INTRODUCTION

We do not know the name of the first master dehydrator, that innovator who recognized that apples left outside in intense sunshine could be saved and eaten later. Their story is old, perhaps as old as Egyptian civilization, and lost in time. However, it is safe to say that drying food as a preservation method has been around for as long as people have been keeping records.

During the Middle Ages, people in Europe built rooms as an extension of distilleries that were specifically designed to dehydrate food by the heat of an indoor fire. Food was strung across the room, smoked, and dried. The lack of sunlight and dry days made it impossible to dry food outside, and these specialty houses solved the problem for people living in a cool, wet climate.

By the mid-1800s, a process was developed so vegetables could be dried at 105°F and compressed into cakes. These dried vegetables were a welcome source of nutrition for sailors who suffered through long voyages without fresh food. During World War II, soldiers used dehydrated food as lightweight rations while serving on the battlefield. We know these today as "meals ready to eat" (MREs). After the war, housewives did not rush to add this compact, but often tasteless, food into their daily cooking routines, and dehydrated food fell out of favor.

We probably have the backpacking community to thank for the modern resurgence of dehydrated food. Their demand for simple, lightweight, and nutritious meals has created a need for prepackaged fruit, vegetables, side dishes and full-course meals, along with a renewed interest in dehydrating machines and other means of drying foods. These new convenience foods can be found at any grocery and outdoor store and are known for their easy preparation and quick cooking time. The taste has improved so much that you would consider it a fine dinner. Modern preppers have taken this challenge a step further by learning to produce, store, and rotate a year's worth of food in their own prepared pantry.

This guidebook teaches you the basics of dehydrating fruit, vegetables, and protein; gives detailed information about drying 50 types of fruits and vegetables; and shares some time-tested and family-loved recipes for everyday use. Everything you need to learn to stock your own healthy, shelf-stable pantry is included.

As a prepper who is also a gardener, I wish to take my pantry preparations beyond beans, rice, wheat, and powdered eggs. Dehydrating my garden bounty fills the gap left by food that can't be canned and a freezer susceptible to power outages. A clean water source and fire are the only things that stand between my family and a hot meal prepared with dehydrated ingredients.

This book is not just for experienced gardeners, conscientious preppers, and expert preservers. It is for anyone who loves fresh food and wants to have a hand in how it is preserved. To accommodate the active lifestyles of today, dehydrating needs to fit easily into your daily routine, take as little time as possible, and require a minimum amount of preparation time. By combining bulk buying with batched preserving sessions, as well as an efficient dehydrator, you can be drying food to use every day.

Anyone can use this book, including:

- **Preppers** who want to create a healthy year's supply of food that is tailor-made for their family's dietary needs.

- **Homesteaders** who have the land to plant additional crops and want to create their own extended pantry supply.

- **Busy families** who want to purchase in bulk and have ingredients for quick, healthy meals at their fingertips.

- **Suburban and urban gardeners** who are trying to grow and preserve their harvest in an efficient way.

- **Parents** who want to replace their children's consumption of sugary and emply-calorie snacks with healthy alternatives.

My dream is that after you learn how to dehydrate, you will see the possibilities for quick, healthy meals and begin to use these techniques every day. May you never waste another orange peel, wilted celery stick, or bag of spinach again!

CHAPTER 1

WHY DEHYDRATE?

Years ago, when I was just beginning to get serious about putting together a food storage plan, my husband and I decided to purchase a side of beef from a local farmer. Our extra chest freezer was in a detached garage about 20 feet from the house, and we loaded it up with all the wonderful cuts we had asked the processor to wrap for us. That chest freezer was full of frozen meat, vegetables, and fruit with enough to last for months and months of homemade meals. It was fantastic—and stupid.

One day I went out to get a roast and found that the kids had rummaged through the freezer several days earlier and the lid had not closed properly. Yep—all the food inside had thawed, and all our hard work and money went down the drain, gone, ruined.

I learned a valuable food storage lesson that day. The rule of three in food preservation is to make sure that you do not put all your eggs in one basket; that is to say, you need to have your food stored in at least three separate ways. Of course, you'll still want to have food in the freezer, but learning to process food in canning jars using a water bath and pressure canner is important too. Dehydrating fills the gap and allows you to have another avenue of properly stored food that has a long-term shelf life.

Since that day we have never had a food storage catastrophe hit us with that much force. We use canning, freezing, and dehydrating to round it all out. If the jars break or the freezer gets left open again, we will not lose all of our food supplies.

Benefits of Dehydrating

One of the reasons I like dehydrating so much is because it is easy, and there is only a small learning curve to get started. Basically, if you can chop food, blanch vegetables, and know what specific food should look like when it is completely dry, you can be successful in adding dehydrated food to your pantry.

Freezer space can be in short supply when you are trying to store a year's reserve of food. Why use that precious space when you can dehydrate the food and maintain the same quality? Dehydrating saves freezer space for more important things in your food storage plan.

Compared to canned food, dehydrated food has a long shelf life. This food, when stored with the oxygen removed, will be edible for at least five years. While home pressure-canned food may lose its color and texture after one or two years, dehydrated food retains its quality. Commercially purchased dehydrated food has an even longer shelf life, sometimes up to 20 years.

Also unlike canning, dehydrating has minimal processing watch time. I can do other things while my food is dehydrating, while I'm pretty much tied to the stove while I'm canning. The chopping time remains the same, but there is no additional time required for watching the pot boil. Once you have the food cut and placed on the dehydrator trays, you can walk away and return hours later to check on the process.

Dehydrated food is portable and weighs less than any other kind of stored food. During processing, 70 to 95 percent of the water is removed from the food. It is the best choice for packing in 72-hour kits and taking on hiking or backpacking trips.

Additionally, dehydrated food tastes great, and the drying process actually intensifies the flavor of the food you produce. Food reconstitutes beautifully with water, juice, or broth, and it will often look and taste like it is freshly cooked. You can easily make your own instant meal packages with dehydrated food. Combine the ingredients into two- to four-person meal portions and store it in Mylar bags with oxygen absorbers. It's easy to reach into the pantry shelves and have a quick meal ready in minutes.

Bulk purchases of food items are less expensive, so when you buy in bulk and dehydrate your own food, you'll save money in the grocery budget over the long term. The cost of food in the United States increased 1.1 percent in July 2017 and is projected to reach 1.9 percent by the year 2020. Bulk purchases and dehydrating give you an edge against food inflation.[1] Have a bag of spinach or lettuce that will not be used before it expires? Just pop it onto a dehydrator tray and preserve it for later. You'll find dozens of ways to preserve food that would otherwise go to waste, saving even more money.

The Prepared Pantry

Do you plan what you are going to do with your garden produce ahead of time? Do you know how many jars of tomato sauce you'll need for the next three months of meals? How about for a year?

To get a prepared pantry, you must purposefully plan your pantry and create an extended supply of food. For some people, that will be a three-month food supply; others will want a supply of food to last a year. This extended stash of food, purchased at the best price or grown yourself, will stave off hardship during an economic downturn just as much as your savings account will. It's best to preserve these items when they are at peak season and when they are at the best price. It's like setting the lowest price on your food to ward off inflation. I've

---

1 Trading Economics, "United States Food Inflation Forecast," accessed November 13, 2017, https://tradingeconomics.com/united-states/food-inflation/forecast.

PREPPER'S **DEHYDRATOR** HANDBOOK

found that if I can save even 20 cents per pound on an item that we eat regularly, it is worth it. What are 20 cents of savings for something you use every day, like yogurt? For a family of four that uses a cup of yogurt every weekday, it adds up to $208 a year. That's $208 that could pay off a debt or purchase other food items.

Begin to fill out your stocked pantry by storing the things that you use all the time. For some families that might be pancake mix, and for others it could be applesauce or cream of mushroom soup. My family always has spicy mustard, a variety of sauces, and salad dressings in our food supply. We could do without then, but why should we? Planning ahead makes it possible.

In order for this to be cost-effective, you should only store what you regularly eat. It isn't a good purchase if it sits on your shelf and goes bad. That can of jellied cranberries that's been sitting in your pantry for the last year is reaching its useful shelf life and will be wasted money. What could you do with it? You could add to its shelf life by adding applesauce and spices to make fruit leather.

For the most prepared pantry, store a combination of frozen food and shelf-stable foods. Use this book and take the time to learn the basics of dehydrating, along with how to freeze fruits and vegetables. Master the art of water bath and pressure canning. As I mentioned earlier, you should always store food in at least three different ways. Then, if a natural disaster comes and knocks out your power for a week, you may lose the contents of your freezer, but you will have dehydrated and canned foods in your pantry. That means you still have food to eat, and the financial loss will not be as great.

Ultimately, making a daily trip to the grocery to get supplies defeats the purpose of a fully stocked pantry, which is to have healthy food at all times and to save money. See the chart on page 8 for pantry items that will get you started on your ultimate prepared pantry.

PANTRY ESSENTIALS

STAPLES	BAKING INGREDIENTS	SPICES AND SEASONING
Cornmeal	Baking chocolate, unsweetened	Allspice
Noodles	Baking powder	Apple cider vinegar
Powdered eggs	Baking soda	Balsamic vinegar
Powdered milk	Condensed milk	Cayenne pepper
Salt	Cornstarch	Cinnamon
Stock (chicken, beef, vegetable, bouillon cubes)	Cream of tartar	Dill
	Evaporated milk	Garlic (fresh and dried)
Sugar	Honey	Lemon juice
Tomato paste, sauce, or powder	Maple extract	Lemon zest or dried lemon peel
	Molasses	Mustard (prepared or seeds)
Wheat or spelt, in grain form	Nuts	
White flour	Powdered sugar	Nutmeg
White rice	Vanilla extract	Onion (powder and diced)
Yeast		Oregano

OILS AND FATS	PROTEIN	Paprika
Butter	Beans, dried or canned	Pepper
Olive oil	Beef, frozen or canned	Rosemary
Shortening	Chicken, frozen or canned	Soy sauce
Vegetable oil		Thyme
	Jerky	Worcestershire sauce
	Tuna, canned	

In addition to the basic staples, you should stock a variety of canned, dehydrated, and frozen fruits and vegetables that you can use to make quick meals and that your family will eat.

Do you have a variety of spices? Our spice cabinet is huge, and I think it's the secret to our pantry. If you have a variety of herbs and spices to use in different combinations, you can create a host of individualized meals. Ground beef can be served several times a week when you have the seasonings to mix up the menu and make unique meals. We purchase our spices in bulk once or twice a year from The San Francisco Herb Company (https://sfherb.com). They have spice blends and individual herbs and spices that I cannot grow at home.

Don't overlook buying canned goods from the store. Most grocery stores have a twice-yearly canned goods sale that allows you to stock up on items you may not be able to purchase or grow yourself.

Purchase meat when it's on sale and wrap it into family portion sizes, or invest in a FoodSaver machine to remove excess oxygen.

One Year of Food Storage for a Family of Four

My pantry is stocked and rotated on the "store what you eat" philosophy, so we preserve and store the food that we like the most. This also helps with meal preparation, and we can reach into the pantry and pull out the ingredients for a home-cooked meal at any time. Dehydrating is not our only preservation method, but it is the one that we lean on the most for food that has a long shelf-stable life. We have well-balanced and nutritious meals available at any time. You can use our basic formula to put together a food storage plan for your family.

Start by tracking what you eat for two weeks. Not just the meals, but the actual ingredients used to make each one. Most families have a set of about 14 basic recipes that they rotate through on a regular basis. Keeping a two-week meal rotation will help to cut out food fatigue (are we having *that* again?) and make rotating your food easier.

Here's an example. Take your favorite spaghetti meal, break it down by ingredients, and put the recipe in a spreadsheet or write on an index card. Note each of the ingredients.

- 1 (16-ounce) box spaghetti

- 1 (15-ounce) can tomato sauce (or 15 ounces homemade sauce)

- 1 pound ground meat or premade frozen meatballs

- 1 tablespoon Italian seasoning

- 1 teaspoon garlic

- ½ cup cheese, shredded

- 1 (8-ounce) box biscuit mix

- 16 ounces fresh fruit

- 16 ounces fresh vegetables

Now, buy enough of each of those shelf-stable items to stock your pantry for a year of that meal (calculating that you will eat the meal twice a month):

- 24 (16-ounce) boxes spaghetti

- 24 (15-ounce) cans tomato sauce (or dehydrated tomato powder equivalent)

- 24 pounds frozen or canned ground beef (or 2 #10 cans freeze-dried beef)

- 24 tablespoons Italian seasoning

- 24 teaspoons garlic

- 12 cups cheese, shredded

- 24 (8-ounce) boxes biscuit mix

- 24 servings dehydrated fruits x the number of people in your family

- 24 servings dehydrated vegetables x the number of people in your family

Does stocking one meal at a time seem daunting? After you have identified the 14 meals your family eats, begin by slowly purchasing individual items during each weekly grocery shopping trip. Start with one month's worth of meals (two times each recipe), two months, or three months, depending on what will fit into your grocery budget.

FOOD STORAGE GUIDELINES FOR 1 ADULT FOR 1 YEAR

COMMODITY	AMOUNT
Grains (cereal, corn, oats, pasta, rice, wheat)	400 pounds
Dairy products (cheese, powdered milk)	30 pounds
Legumes (dried beans, lentils, nuts, peas)	60 pounds
Sweeteners (brown sugar, honey, molasses, sugar, syrup)	60 pounds
Leavening agents (applesauce, baking powder, baking soda, powdered eggs, yeast)	6 pounds
Salt (bouillon cubes, sea salt, soy sauce, table salt)	6 pounds
Fats (butter, shortening, vegetable oil)	30 pounds
Fruit (before processing)	200 pounds
Vegetables (before processing)	200 pounds
Meat (beef, chicken, fish, pork, turkey, etc.)	100 pounds

Do this for each of the meals that you have identified over that two-week period. Every breakfast, lunch, dinner, and snack should be accounted for. This method allows you to track what you already eat, helps you to break it down by ingredients, and allows you to plan out the specific number of months you want your pantry to serve. It also helps to know how many pounds of fresh fruit and vegetables will need to be dehydrated each year in order to supply the meals you eat. It is highly customizable, so you can modify it specifically for your exact needs.

You may find that breakfast and lunch do not need to be rotated as frequently as dinners. Most of us are fine with eating yogurt, cereal, eggs, or toast and jam several times a week. Start with five to seven of these recipes, but keep dinners on a longer rotation schedule.

You can get basic recommendations for the amounts of protein, carbs, fruit, vegetables, grains, and calories to store by visiting the food storage calculator at ProvidentLiving.com, which has been adapted into a reference chart above.[2] Don't let the chart be that last word on what to store, however; you know what your family likes to eat, and you may find that your family eats more fruits and vegetables than is suggested. Note: One serving of fresh fruits or vegetables is about 4 ounces. However, each fresh fruit or vegetable dehydrates differently. Reference Chapter 9 to see how fresh fruits and vegetables convert to their dehydrated forms to get a more accurate idea of serving sizes.

---

2 Provident Living, "Food Storage Calculator," accessed November 13, 2017, http://providentliving.com/preparedness/food-storage/foodcalc.

CHAPTER 2

DEHYDRATING METHODS

Harness the Sun

Drying food by sunlight has been practiced for hundreds of years and works best for those living in a hot, dry climate. It is not recommended for those living in colder, damp, northern climates. Even those living in the South have too much humidity for success. The optimal temperature is between 90°F and 100°F, with less than 60 percent humidity.

If those conditions fit your climate, create a series of drying racks from old picture frames by covering them with window screening or cotton sheeting. Tack the screens to the bottom of the frames with staples. Think about the food safety of the materials you are using and plan accordingly. The screens should be safe for contact with food, so avoid hardware cloth or other materials that are coated with galvanized metal and can be found at the home improvement store. Choose, instead, stainless steel, Teflon-coated fiberglass, or plastic. These materials will clean nicely and not oxidize when they are exposed to the sun.

Place the food you are drying on the screens and set the prepared frames in full sunlight for several days until the food is dry. Airflow is important for success. The trays can be stacked with wooden blocks between them to aid the process. Cover the food with cheesecloth to keep pests away during the drying time. Bring the racks in at night before the dew falls, or if there is excessive wind or it looks like it might rain. You don't want all your hard work to be undone.

For those that are living off-grid, solar drying may be your only option. Several plans can be found online for creating an enclosed solar box dehydrator. The enclosed-box drying method is less susceptible to humidity than regular solar methods and, compared with sun drying on racks, the temperature is higher and drying time is shorter. These appear to be relatively easy to make using salvaged materials around your home. Search "solar dehydrator box" or "solar dehydrator plans" in your favorite search engine for ideas.

In the Oven

Dehydrating in the oven is perhaps the most inefficient way to preserve your food because you need to keep your oven door open during the process. Oven drying takes two or three times longer than drying in a dehydrator and has a higher energy cost. While it does produce a safe and tasty product, the quality is different from food prepared in an electric dehydrator. Oven-dried food is more brittle and usually darker and less flavorful than food dried in a dehydrator. Don't let this deter you; an oven will work in a pinch if it is all you have. It requires little or no investment in equipment.

Test your oven temperature with a thermometer before you use it to dry food. Set the oven to the lowest temperature setting and prop open the door for one hour. The oven should maintain a temperature of between 130° to 150°F. If the oven does not maintain the temperature range, your finished product will begin to cook instead of dry. Conversely, if the temperature is too cool, you run the risk of food spoilage.

Here are some tips for oven drying:

- Use your oven to dry small amounts of food at a time. If you overload the oven, the drying time will be extended.

- Position the oven rack at its lowest setting.

- Prepare the food as recommended (see meat recommendations in Chapter 7, and fruit and vegetable recommendations in Chapter 9) and place it on a cookie sheet, or place cotton sheeting directly on the wire rack.

- Prop the door open with a wooden spoon or block of wood; you'll need airflow for this to be successful.

- Set a timer for one hour, check for dryness, and turn the food.

- Repeat every hour until the food is dry.

Using a Dehydrator

Years ago I purchased an old Ronco dehydrator at a garage sale for just a few bucks. It has 10 trays, no motor, and uses radiant bottom heat to dry the food. I thought I was in heaven. This machine is considered a dinosaur by today's fancy dehydrator standards, but I still have it and use it every year when I'm drying herbs. I love how quiet it is.

My next garage sale treasure was a Harvest Maid Dehydrator with a box of four extra trays. I have used that machine for years, creating all the things you read about in this book. It has an electric motor and blower at the base of the unit. Seriously, I've used these second-hand machines for at least 15 years. They are workhorses and prove that you don't need a fancy machine to have a prepared pantry.

Today's electric dehydrators make your pantry preservation even easier, and they run more efficiently than those old machines. In addition, many new machines have a timer to allow you to start and stop drying when it suits your schedule, and their 1000-watt heaters get the job done in record time. There are three basic dehydrator designs on the market today.

TYPES OF DEHYDRATORS

Dehydrators need to circulate air in order to do their job. This is accomplished by pushing air vertically through the machine, either from the bottom or the top, or by circulating air from the side horizontally.

Older model vertical airflow dehydrators have a heating element and fan located at the base of the unit, and the trays are stacked on top. This was the golden standard for years, and with a moving motor, it's a step up from my old Ronco machine. The one drawback to these old airflow machines is that the food does not dry evenly on the trays. The trays always need to be rotated from the top of the stack to the bottom to ensure each tray gets equal airflow. That can be a problem if you were hoping to load the machine and walk away until the food is dry.

In modern dehydrators, vertical airflow is accomplished by having a powerful motor at the top of the stack. This allows for a cleaner heating element and forces heated, pressurized air downward through the outer ring of the food trays. These machines are very efficient. At the same time, the circulating air moves horizontally across each tray and out through the bottom, and the air converges at the center for fast, even drying. I've found that with my Nesco Gardenmaster machine, there's no need to rotate trays—all the food dehydrates at the same time and it can handle up to 20 trays. You can efficiently dry a lot of food at one time.

Excalibur is the gold standard of horizontal airflow dehydrator units; it is also the most expensive. The heating element and fan are located in the back of the machine and provide horizontal airflow, which is said to reduce flavor mixing when you are dehydrating several different foods at one time. All trays receive equal heat distribution, and because cool air is drawn in, heated, and distributed evenly over each tray, the food dries faster and retains more nutrients, without tray rotation. If you are going to dry a lot of jerky, soup, or fruit leather, a dehydrator with horizontal airflow may be the best choice.

I now own five different dehydrators, including a Nesco Gardenmaster and an Excalibur 9-tray model. Each one, old and new, is regularly used for different drying purposes. You don't need a dehydrator to dry food, but it sure does make it easier and more efficient.

When you are drying large batches, it is helpful to have more than one dehydrator. The machine with bottom heat dries my herbs; it is the least precise of the machines and the one that needs tray rotation. It works well for herbs because they are not prone to spoiling, like some fruit or vegetables that need constant airflow. The Nesco Gardenmaster top-heat machine makes terrific work of fruit and vegetables, and I've found that there is very little tray rotation that needs to take place. It has digital time and heat instruments so I can schedule time in half-hour stages and adjust the temperature in 5°F increments. The Excalibur machine is square and is perhaps a more efficient use of tray space. With horizontal heating from the back, it makes excellent jerky and leathers.

Which one should you choose, horizontal or vertical airflow? It really is a personal preference. Any of the machines on the market today will dry food. I suggest you start with a machine that fits your budget and then expand to a large-capacity machine if you need to.

DEHYDRATOR BASICS

As a general rule, food should not be touching as it dries on dehydrator trays. This additional space aids with airflow and will help to dry your product fast and evenly. Also, juicy fruits like strawberries, mango, or watermelon will stick together when drying if they touch on the trays. The exception to this rule is leafy vegetables like cabbage, lettuce, spinach, or cilantro. They can be added to trays up to ½-inch thick, although you will need to reach in every few hours and stir the leaves.

If you have a machine with bottom heat, it is often necessary to aid your machine with air circulation by rotating the trays from top to bottom. Set a timer for halfway through the drying process and move the top tray to the bottom, shuffling each tray as you go. When finished, the original tray on the top will now be on the bottom of the stack. If you have a machine with horizontal airflow, rotate the trays 90 degrees halfway through the process. As you use your machine more often, you'll get to know its ins and outs and how much help it needs with airflow.

There are many variables in food dehydration. Humidity, methods of food handling, and different kinds of produce will change the quality of your dried food each time you make a batch. The only way to become an expert is to keep experimenting until you understand how each of the items you wish to store in your pantry will behave. Fortunately, dehydrating is a forgiving preservation method.

TIPS FOR DEHYDRATOR DRYING

Try different methods. Don't be afraid to experiment with different dehydration methods. Vary the way you make cuts and the thickness of the foods you use. Julienne a potato at least one time to see how it turns out.

Set aside a small portion of a product to test pretreatment recommendations. Pretreatments can be a hassle and are not always necessary. Experiment with using a pretreatment dip or blanch and compare that to not using a pretreatment process at all so you can see how the finished product meets your needs and preferences. Keep records so you remember which is preferred.

Spread food evenly, in single layers, on trays. Unless you're drying leafy greens, overlapping items will take longer to dry and might stick together.

Separate foods by their thicknesses on dehydrator trays. Take green onions, for instance. Each stalk has a dark green and a white portion, which dry at different rates. If you keep them all mixed together on a tray, you'll need to pick out the dry green portions after a few hours. If you separate pieces by the thickness at the beginning, you can just remove the finished tray of greens when they are done. It will save you a lot of energy if you plan ahead.

Do not mix fresh items in with those in the process of dehydrating. Don't add fresh food to a partially dried batch; it will slow the drying time on all the trays.

Consolidate partially dried foods onto fewer trays. Halfway through the process, combine partially dried foods onto fewer trays. Keep in mind that modern machines are most efficient if they operate with at least four trays. If you don't have four trays of food to dry, be sure to add empty trays to the stack to help with airflow.

Do not start and stop the dehydration process. Dehydrating works by continually moving heated air over your food, which helps prevent spoiling and off flavors. Each item needs to dry continually for the recommended time. You don't want the heat to stop on a partially dried batch, so make sure timers are set to continue the process overnight while you sleep.

Microwave Drying

Microwave drying is not recommended for fruit, vegetables, and meat because of the uneven way they cook. All microwaves are designed to retain the moisture content in foods, not as a method of drying them. Also, fruits have high sugar content and will have a tendency to burn if they are overcooked in the microwave.

If you are determined to use your microwave for dehydrating, follow these rules:

1. Cut food no more than ¼ inch thick.

2. Lay the product directly on the turnstile.

3. Dry in small batches.

4. Do not overlap food.

5. Use the defrost setting (reduced power) to minimize the hardening effect that can happen when food is dried too quickly.

6. Turn the food every 15 minutes until it has dried to the consistency you are looking for.

Microwave drying is not a process where you can push the button and step away, unlike drying with an electric dehydrator. You must constantly monitor the batch to make sure the food does not get too dry, burn, and catch fire. And it *will* catch fire if you do not watch it continually!

For the best success, skip the fruit, and use the microwave to dehydrate only herbs or leafy greens. These contain a very minimal amount of moisture and are best suited for microwave drying. Place washed and towel-dried herbs on a paper towel or napkin and dry in 30-second increments until they reach the consistency you are looking for. See Chapter 8 about drying herbs for more information.

CHAPTER 3

BASIC DEHYDRATING INSTRUCTIONS

Learning to dehydrate gives you a tremendous variety of food that can be stored in your prepared pantry. Fortunately, there is room for creativity in the process. There is more than one way to prepare food for processing, but each fruit and vegetable is treated differently. This chapter will discuss small- and large-batch processing, how to pretreat food using blanching and oxidizing techniques, and how to store the food once you have it dried.

Keep these tips, applicable to all methods of dehydrating, in mind as you begin:

- **Clean your produce.** Thoroughly clean each piece of produce. This is especially important if you are not buying or growing organic.

- **Use fresh, ripe produce.** Choose fruit and vegetables at their peak freshness. Items that are underripe will not have a good flavor. Overripe fruit can still be used when making fruit leather.

- **Cut pieces evenly.** Use a mandoline or salad chopper to achieve evenly cut pieces; this helps with faster drying times.

- **Group similarly sized pieces on the same tray.** The size of the piece to be dehydrated is important; for even drying, keep all like sizes and thicknesses together on the trays.

Supplies

BASIC SUPPLIES

One of the best things about dehydrating food is how simple it is. Only a few basic supplies are needed for success, and most of them are already in your kitchen.

- cutting board

- drying racks

- heat source (dehydrator, the sun, an oven)

- jars, for storage

- plastic fruit leather trays or plastic wrap

- pot, for blanching

- sharp knife

- slotted spoon

- strainer to wash produce

ADDITIONAL SUPPLIES

Once you become proficient at dehydrating, you'll find ways to incorporate dry food into all of your food preparations. After a while, I looked for time-saving items to help the process along and have added several other supplies to my food drying "kit."

Here are some other tools that make quick work of cutting, chopping, and pureeing. You might want to purchase them as budget allows:

- 100cc oxygen absorbers
- apple peeler/corer—once you use one, you'll never process an apple by hand again!
- blender or food processor
- canning funnels—handy for transferring dried items into jars
- food-grade buckets for long-term storage of all supplies
- mandoline slicer, to quickly give you uniform and specialty cuts for soft and hard vegetables
- Paraflexx trays
- salad shooter, for soft vegetables like zucchini and tomatoes
- vacuum sealer and bags
- vegetable brush, to scrub root vegetables clean
- vegetable peelers, to save your fingers from sharp knives

None of these extended supplies are necessary, but they are handy to have if you are doing large batches of food processing and if you want to extend the shelf life. Having them around can make a long job go quickly and allow you to process more food. Start with the least expensive items and purchase others as you increase your skills.

Dehydrating in Small Batches

Today's dehydrators are so economical to use that you can afford to have one running on the counter at all times. They are terrific for preserving the last of the spinach bag or apples that will not get eaten before they start to turn. Anything can be dehydrated in small batches. Recently, I purchased several bundles of cilantro for homemade salsa and found that there were two large handfuls left over. Rather than making another batch of salsa or putting the cilantro in the compost pile, I cleaned the leaves, trimmed the stems, and processed two trays. This was ground into powder and will later be used to flavor sauces and dip. Use these tips to dehydrate small batches of food.

- Most dehydrators need proper airflow to do their job and work best with at least four trays. If you don't have four trays of food, alternate full and blank trays to make the required number.

- Cut the food into uniform sizes to aid with uniform drying times.

- It's alright to have trays with different food items, but steer clear of mixing onion or garlic with other types of food; their flavors will taint the food on the other trays.

Dehydrating in Large Batches

When I can't grow enough of my own, I like to purchase large quantities of in-season fruit and vegetables from the local farmers produce stand. This lets me quickly stock my pantry. Large-batch dehydrating can be an all-day task and requires some stamina to get the job done.

Produce growers have standardized the way they package their product, so if you want to purchase fruit or veggies in bulk from the local market, they will sell it to you (often at a discount) in 40-pound boxes. That is a lot of produce to wash, cut, treat for oxidizing, and place on dehydrating trays, so it's good to do so efficiently. Here are some tips for processing larger batches of dehydrated food.

- Processing is easier if you break it into stations. Set up a cleaning station, cutting station, and blanching or oxidizing station to make the best use of your space.

- Consider purchasing tools to speed up the processing. Using a mandoline slicer or food processor will make the cutting job go faster and give you uniform pieces.

- Plan ahead and know which cuts you will be making. A 40-pound box of apples can be made into chips, diced for baking, or turned into applesauce and dried.

- Make sure you have enough dehydrators to hold the produce. Borrow from friends if necessary.

- Set up a conditioning and packaging area, so dried food can get stored as soon as possible.

- Get help from friends and family. Teach the next generation how fun it is as they learn to dry their own food.

Blanching Vegetables for Dehydrating

Each vegetable has its own rule to follow before being placed in the freezer or dehydrator, and you should know the rules before you decide if you want to break them. Some vegetables need to be blanched, others might need to be blanched, and some should be left alone.

When you blanch vegetables, you boil or steam them for a few minutes, then quickly cool them in ice water. Each vegetable has a different time requirement for blanching, usually from two to five minutes. This process stops the enzyme activity that causes plants to lose nutrients and change texture once they are frozen.

Blanched vegetables can be placed directly onto dehydrator trays and processed for the proper time.

No-blanch vegetables. Several vegetable crops freeze or dry well and do not require blanching at all. These are my favorites, because they are so easy to get into the pantry! They can be washed and halved, quartered, or chopped, then towel dried and placed directly in the dehydrator for processing. Do not wash mushrooms; it will cause them to discolor. Instead, wipe the mushrooms clean with a towel. For herbs and leafy greens (such as parsley, cilantro, and spinach), cut leaves with stems several inches long. Tie in bunches and swish in cold water to wash, then towel dry.

BLANCHING FRUIT AND VEGETABLES

NEVER	MAYBE	ALWAYS
Apples	Asparagus (½-inch pieces or smaller)	Asparagus (larger than ½-inch pieces; whole)
Apricots	Carrots (diced)	Beets
Bananas	Cauliflower	Broccoli
Berries	Celery	Chickpeas
Cabbage	Cherries	Carrots (sliced; whole)
Citrus	Eggplant	Corn
Coconuts	Figs	Grapes
Cucumbers	Ginger	Green beans (whole)
Garlic	Green beans (French sliced; 1-inch pieces)	Green peas (in pod)
Herbs	Green peas (no pod)	Parsnips (larger pieces)
Horseradish	Onions	Plums
Kiwis	Peaches	Peanuts
Leafy greens	Nectarines	Potatoes
Leeks	Parsnips (diced)	Rhubarb
Mangoes	Pears	Tomatoes, fresh
Melons		Yams
Mushrooms		Winter squash
Papayas		
Peppers		
Pineapples		
Summer squash		
Tomatoes, frozen		

Maybe-blanch vegetables. Some crops *may* require blanching. These usually call for minimal blanching time in boiling water, and you may find that you'll have great success skipping it all together. The texture of these foods when they are rehydrated remains good for soups, stews, and casseroles. These have a storage life up to one year, so it is best only to prepare what you will use in that time frame and continually rotate your supplies.

The key to being able to skip the blanching on these vegetables is the way you cut them before processing. If the pieces are small enough, that you can usually skip the step. These vegetables should be thoroughly cleaned, chopped, and towel dried to get out any excess moisture.

The process for dehydrating is simple. Place the vegetables in a single layer on dehydrator sheets and process according to individual temperatures and times. After drying, store in canning jars in a cool dark place.

Always-blanch vegetables. Some vegetables will always require blanching before you store them in your freezer or process them in the dehydrator. You should only use vegetables that are in excellent condition.

SET UP A BLANCHING STATION

If you find blanching vegetables as distasteful as I do, consider creating a blanching station to make the process go a bit faster. Begin by making an assembly line from your stovetop to your sink.

You'll need a stockpot, several clean towels, cold water, a bag of ice, and a sieve for removing the vegetables from the pot.

1. Bring a stockpot filled with water to a rolling boil.

2. Fill your kitchen sink or a tub insert with cold water and ice.

3. Place a small batch of vegetables in the boiling water for the recommended time and promptly remove it to the cold water bath using the sieve.

4. Once the blanched vegetables are cooled, remove from the water and place on a kitchen towel to pat dry.

5. Process for drying on dehydrator trays.

You will find that the water in the stockpot will need to be replenished a few times during the process and that you will need to add ice to keep the cool water cold.

Fruit Pretreatments to Prevent Oxidization

Certain fruits turn brown when they are exposed to the air for too long. You can probably name a few, including apples, bananas, pears, and peaches. Pretreating the fruit before drying will keep it from turning color, and may help retain nutrients and texture. This process is not necessary, and if you decide to skip it, you will still have a tasty finished product. Keep in mind that if you skip pretreatments, the fruit may not look the way your family expects it to look, and they may be less inclined to eat it.

Two types of pretreatments may be used on fruit: dipping in a solution and steam blanching.

FRUIT DIPPING

Dehydrating is not an exact science, and there is room for your own interpretation when dehydrating fruit. Which should you choose, honey dip, lemon juice, or ascorbic acid? I would recommend trying fruit using each type of dip and then make a batch with none at all. You may find that the whole process is not important for your family.

Ascorbic acid or citric acid (vitamin C) dip. Vitamin C and ascorbic acid can be found in the pharmacy or in the canning aisle of your local grocery store. This method does not leave an aftertaste on the fruit.

To make the solution: Mix 2 tablespoons of powder with 1 quart water. Soak the fruit in small batches for 2 to 3 minutes. Remove with a slotted spoon and let dry before placing on dehydrator trays.

Fruit juice dip. Pineapple, lemon, and lime have naturally occurring citric acid, and the juice makes a fine pretreatment, but it is less effective than using ascorbic acid. Dipping in juice may add a slight flavor to the fruit.

To make the solution: Stir 1 cup juice into 1 quart warm water and soak fruit in small batches for 10 minutes. Remove with a slotted spoon and let dry before placing on dehydrator trays.

Honey dip. If you choose a honey dip, it will make the fruit sweeter and add extra calories. This will give you the consistency of store-bought dehydrated fruit, which your children may prefer.

To make the solution: Dissolve 1 cup sugar in 3 cups hot water. Let it cool until it is barely warm and stir in 1 cup honey. Dip fruit in small batches, remove with a slotted spoon, and drain thoroughly before placing on dehydrator sheets. This fruit will stick to your trays, so consider using parchment paper or non-stick dehydrator tray covers.

BLANCHING

Steam blanching. Most fruits are too delicate to be boiled and still retain their shape. Instead, to prevent oxidation, steam the cut fruit pieces in batches for 1 minute, then remove to an ice water dip and drain thoroughly before placing on trays.

Boil blanching. Some fruits need to be fully blanched first to prepare the outside skin for drying, which improves the texture and drying time of the finished product. These include apricots, blueberries, cranberries, gooseberries, currants, grapes (raisins), and plums (prunes). These fruits simply have to be placed in a colander, dipped in boiling water for 30 seconds, then cooled in ice water and drained.

There is one important thing to remember with these pretreatment dips: Your fruit must be as dry as possible before beginning the dehydrating process. If you add wet fruit to the trays, you will significantly increase the drying time of each batch.

Food Touching on Trays

There is a significant difference between drying herbs, vegetables, and fruit. You may wonder if fresh items can touch on the tray as they are drying. Follow these general rules:

Herbs and leafy greens. Herbs and leafy greens can be placed in piles on the drying trays. Their low water content will keep them from sticking together, and they will dry fast. Pick out the dried leaves every hour, mix up the remaining leaves, and continue processing until all are finished.

Vegetables. Most vegetables can be placed close together on drying trays and can touch each other. If you are using the proper drying temperature of 125° to 135°F, they will reduce in size fairly quickly and still have enough room for airflow. They will not stick together when drying. Again, pick out dried pieces every few hours and allow the rest to continue drying.

Fruits. Due to the high sugar content of most fruits, fruits should be placed on drying trays in a single layer without any pieces touching. Any pieces that touch will dry together in one piece and perhaps even stick to the tray while they dry. Use tray covers or parchment paper to reduce the amount of sticking, and turn pieces every few hours as needed.

Conditioning the Finished Product

Properly dried fruit will have a moisture content of 20 percent. Since those doing home food production do not have a way to measure the moisture content, we use a conditioning process to equalize the moisture in the finished product. Conditioning ensures that all the pieces of fruit have dried evenly, and it helps to prevent mold and bacteria from growing during storage. This should be done before packaging for long-term storage.

1. Take the cooled, dried fruit and pack it loosely in glass canning jars. Make sure there is enough room for movement when the jar is shaken.

2. Cap the jar tightly and shake it daily for seven days.

3. Check for moisture condensation. Return any pieces showing moisture to the dehydrator to continue drying.

4. Once the process is complete, proceed with regular packaging. Instructions can be found in Chapter 5.

If you find that pieces have begun to grow mold, they must be thrown away; there is no way to save them.

General Rehydrating Techniques

Dehydrated food is often hard, brittle, and looks somewhat unappealing. Once you introduce water back into it, you'll be surprised how quickly and thoroughly the food returns to its original shape. Not all pieces of dehydrated food can be rehydrated using these methods. Most fruits make great snacks and are eaten dried. Some vegetables are eaten as chips or used in powdered spice mixes instead of rehydrated.

SOAK

Soaking is the easiest, and also the slowest, way to rehydrate food. Place a measured amount of dried food in a bowl and soak it in an equal amount of water until it reaches the desired plumpness, usually 10 to 30 minutes. Pour off any water that is not incorporated back into the food.

Fruit should be soaked in cool water. Vegetables can be soaked in cool, warm, or even boiling water. For a taste variation, consider soaking in juice or broth and then, instead of pouring off the additional liquid, add it directly to the recipe.

Be sure to follow the individual rehydrating requirements for each item found in Chapter 9.

As a general rule, if you will be soaking food for up to an hour, you can do it on the kitchen counter. If you are getting things ready early in the day and plan to use the food during dinner, place the bowl in the refrigerator while it is soaking. It will only absorb as much liquid as it needs and you can pour off any remaining. Refrigeration will prevent spoilage and contamination. Food should never be on the counter for longer than two hours without being refrigerated.

SPRAY

Sometimes delicate fruit only needs to be sprayed with water in order to start plumping back to its original shape. Place the food in a shallow bowl or on a plate and spray until water droplets form on the food. Allow the water to soak in, and keep spraying until the fruit returns to its original shape. Keep a spray bottle handy in the kitchen and give this a try.

SIMMER OR COOK

I like to add dehydrated vegetables to my morning scrambled eggs. Rather than taking the time to rehydrate everything before using it, I place it all in a skillet with just enough water to cover and simmer for five minutes. Once the water has evaporated, they are plumped up, and I'm ready to add the eggs.

Some food does not need to rehydrate before being added to a recipe. When making soup, you can add dried corn, beans, broccoli, cauliflower, or peas directly to the pot and then add additional broth or water to keep your soup at the desired thickness.

Record Keeping

When you are learning to dehydrate different kinds of food for the first time, or when you haven't done it in a while, it is helpful to be able to look back on the process you used before. Record keeping is the key. It will improve your dehydrating techniques and save you a lot of trial and error the next time you want to dry an item. This can be accomplished with a card file or in a spreadsheet on your computer.

Here are some things that you might want to track:

- Date dried

- Quantity dried (e.g., 12 apples)

- Weight of produce before drying (e.g., 6 pounds)

- Weight of produce after drying (e.g., 2 pounds)

- Humidity percent on day of drying

- Drying temperature

- Drying time

- Packaging used

- Special conditioning

- Use-by date

- Preparation method, including:

  » Cut used (julienne, fry cut, crinkle cut, waffle cut, diced, etc.)

  » Cut thickness

  » Quantity and type of spices used

  » Blanching or oxidizing process used

- Additional notes: how it turned out, what you would change next time

CHAPTER 4

FOOD PURCHASING AND SAFETY INFORMATION

The process of dehydrating is rather simple, and you might be tempted to jump right in and get started without taking safety considerations into account. After all, how difficult can it be to dehydrate an apple? That's the beauty of dehydrating your own food. It's not difficult at all, so it's easy to make that extra effort to make sure your food is safe to eat. If you choose the best produce, clean it properly, make sure it is conditioned for storage, and steer clear of a few trouble items, you will have a fully stocked pantry before you know it.

Select the Best Produce

Fresh fruit and vegetables will produce the best final results. If you can purchase from a farmers market or grow your own fruits and vegetables, even better.

Fruit. Begin by choosing firm fruit that is at the peak of ripeness and flavor. Handle it gently to reduce the possibility of bruising, and process it as soon as possible after you bring it home. If you find some of the fruit has become bruised or is overripe by the time you get to it, process it as fruit leather.

Vegetables. Vegetables will be ready for dehydrating when they are fresh, tender, and mature. Process them as soon as possible after harvest. Immature vegetables will have poor color and flavor and after they are rehydrated, they will not have the fresh taste you are seeking. Avoid overly mature vegetables, which can get fibrous. As with fruit, overripe vegetables can be turned into leather, which can be used in soup as a flavoring and thickening agent.

Clean Fruit and Vegetables

Every mother would strive to feed her family only the freshest, organic produce available because no one wants to introduce chemicals and pesticides into their children's daily meals. Unfortunately, purchasing organic produce is not always easy on your budget. You may also find that you have access to large quantities of fresh produce, but it is not organic. Fortunately, there is an option for cleaning fruit and vegetables that do get sprayed with chemicals. You can clean off more than 95 percent of pesticides if you are diligent in this process.

I first learned this technique from Daisy Luther on her blog *The Organic Prepper*. These instructions are adapted from her book, *The Prepper's Canning Guide*.

Use this process for cleaning all of your fruit and vegetables before processing them for dehydrating. Not only does it remove pesticides and traces of fertilizer, but it also removes plain old dirt. It may add an extra step, but it's worth it. The best part of all is that you already have these items in your pantry.

1. Put 1 cup baking soda and a squirt of all-natural dish soap into a sink or tub full of hot water. For more delicate produce, like berries, use cool water.

2. Soak the produce in the solution for about 20 minutes. You may see an alarming white film of gunk rise to the top of the water. That means it is working and the vegetables are getting clean.

3. Drain the sink and rinse the produce. Sturdy produce can be rinsed under a steady stream of water. For delicate produce, scrub your sink or tub clean, fill it with cool fresh water, and swish the produce around in the clean water to rinse it.

4. Using a cloth, scrub the outside of thick-skinned, firm produce like apples. Let delicate produce drain in a colander.

5. If you are still able to see a film or if the rinse water is cloudy, clean out the sink with white vinegar and repeat.

LEAFY GREENS WASH

Leafy greens like lettuce, spinach, and cilantro can be a problem to clean thoroughly, and according to the CDC, they are more likely to be contaminated with E. coli bacteria. This natural wash was found to kill 98 percent of bacteria on produce. It's simple to do, and uses materials straight from your pantry.

Mix 3 cups cool water and 1 cup distilled white vinegar in a bowl or shallow tub. Allow your greens to soak in the bowl for about two minutes, and then rinse them well.

What Not to Dehydrate

Dehydrating is so easy that you might be tempted to throw everything that you like to eat into your machine. However, for safety reasons, there are a few items that are not recommended. Others take so long to process that it is better to purchase them from professionals instead of trying it yourself. Overall, it is better to err on the side of caution when you are dealing with these items.

Eggs. You can find plenty of preppers online that will give you instructions for dehydrating eggs. I'm not one of them. Raw eggs need to be stored at a temperature under 45°F to prevent salmonella poisoning, so in my mind, that means you shouldn't let raw eggs sit on a dehydrator tray for 10 to 12 hours as they are processing.

Other bloggers cook their eggs first, process them for drying, and then powder them. I've heard that there is a consistency issue with these eggs and that you will never get them to rehydrate properly without being grainy. In my opinion, your best bet is to purchase powdered eggs from the professionals. A #10 size container will cost around $35 and will be well worth the investment. Those eggs will provide you with a whole year of eggs for use in baking, plus you'll never have to wonder if you are going to make your family sick.

Foods high in fat. These are not good candidates for dehydrating. High-fat foods don't tend to dry well and are prone to spoilage. Just like eggs, these items are dehydrated or freeze-dried by professionals and are readily available for purchase online. Don't take the risk of doing it yourself. High-fat items to steer clear of include butter, cheese, and avocado.

Meat and fish. Always use extra care when dehydrating any meat products. It's best to store dried meats (even jerky) in the refrigerator or freezer, so why take up the precious storage space? You'll have better success with meat and fish if you store them using the pressure canning method. They will be good for a year, completely shelf stable, and you can pour them right out of the jar for a quick meal.

Jerky is the only exception. Choose a lean cut of raw meat, as free from fat as possible, and dry or brine cure the batch for 6 to 12 hours. The finished product can be stored in vacuum-sealed bags for added shelf life. We'll discuss the details of making your own jerky in Chapter 7.

Milk. It's hard to keep milk inside dehydrator trays, and the whole process tends to be messy. Really, the amount of time it takes to get a small amount of powdered milk is not worth it in the long run. After all, it's mostly water. Purchase whole powdered milk from the professionals; it's a better use of your money and time.

The bottom line is this: Even though food may show up on a do-not-dehydrate list, it doesn't mean that it can't be dehydrated; rather, the time, effort, potential risk, and long-term storage options make it not worth doing. If you're looking to build a long-term pantry, focus on the quick success of dehydrating fruit and vegetables and learn to make jerky. They will build your pantry fast.

The Effects of Light, Oxygen, Heat, and Humidity on Dried Food

I live in the South, in Central Texas, but I'm a transplant from the North. Most Northerners won't have to deal with humidity for most of the year, but if you live in the South, it can be an issue for months on end. The humid time of the year also tends to coincide with harvest time, so there are special considerations for dehydrating food in a humid climate.

According to the article "Drying Food" published by the University of Illinois, College of Agriculture, "The higher the temperature and the lower the humidity, the more rapid the rate of dehydration will be. Humid air slows down evaporation. Keep this in mind if you plan to dry food on hot, muggy summer days."[3]

The process of dehydrating helps moisture escape food through evaporation. Without proper ventilation, humid air trapped in a

---

3 Judy Troftgruben, "Drying Food," University of Illinois at Urbana-Champaign College of Agriculture, April 1984, http://www.aces.uiuc.edu/vista/html_pubs/DRYING/dryfood.html.

dehydrator soon takes on as much moisture as it can hold, and then drying can no longer take place. For this reason, be sure there is plenty of ventilation around your food dryer. The food will dry faster and use less energy when there is sufficient airflow.

If you live in a humid climate, you will also need to package your dried produce as quickly as possible. Take it from my experience: If you leave your dried tomatoes on the counter overnight in a humid house, they will need to be reprocessed a second time the next day. Think of dehydrated food as a moisture sponge; it loves to absorb liquid and humidity. It can easily absorb moisture from the atmosphere and become less dry and susceptible to mold. We'll talk all about how to avoid this with packaging and storage in Chapter 5.

Light, heat, and oxygen are the three elements most likely to reduce the shelf life of dehydrated foods. Here are a few general rules:

- Displaying canning jars full of processed food on an open shelf looks pretty, but it is a surefire way to undermine all the hard work you've done. Always keep your food in a cool, dark, dry cabinet to ensure the longest shelf life.

- Storage temperature helps determine the length of storage. With proper packaging, most dried food can be stored for one year at 60°F and six months at 80°F.

- Pack foods in amounts that can be used all at once. Every time you open a package, you introduce moisture and air that can lower the quality of the food.

- Check dried foods regularly during storage to see if they are still dry. Glass containers work well for this; moisture that collects on the sides is easy to see.

- Discard all food that has developed an off smell or shows signs of mold.

- If the dehydrated food shows signs of moisture and the food has not spoiled, you can use it immediately, or reprocess and repackage it.

There is one final thing to be aware of as you are drying food. It's called "case hardening." You may be tempted to turn up the heat on the dehydrator, quickly remove the moisture, and get the job done. After all, it stands to reason that taking moisture out of the food more quickly will use less energy, right? Unfortunately, it doesn't work that way. If drying takes place too fast, the cells on the outside of the food will give up moisture faster than the cells on the inside. The surface will become hard, preventing the escape of moisture from the inside, and it will take even longer for food to dry. And if you turn up the heat too much, you'll cook your food instead of dehydrating it.

Using Frozen Vegetables

If you do not have access to a large garden or farmers market, consider purchasing frozen vegetables for dehydrating. These vegetables can often be purchased in large bags, and I find them to be an economical choice. Be on the lookout for grocery coupons for even bigger savings.

There is no need to blanch frozen vegetables; this was done by the processor before freezing. That's a quick win for your pantry, because all frozen vegetables can be placed right on the food dehydrator trays with no additional preparation. You don't even need to thaw them. Just throw the bag on the countertop a few times to break up any frozen clumps. If you find that there is residual ice in spots, place those clumps in a kitchen or paper towel and give them a good rubbing. The ice crystals will be absorbed by the towel, and the product is ready for dehydrating. Processing times range from 6 to 16 hours. Follow the suggested dehydrating times found in the description for each vegetable in Chapter 9.

These vegetables dehydrate well from a frozen state:

• Broccoli

• Carrots

• Cauliflower

- Corn

- Okra

- Peas

- Vegetable mix (baby lima beans, carrots, corn, green beans, peas)

A word of caution: Look for vegetables that have been frozen in their most natural state. Any bags that have added sauce or oil are not suitable for dehydrating and should not be used. You'll also find that some manufacturers add sugar to their vegetables. Look closely at the ingredients, and decide if this fits your food storage plans.

Using Frozen Fruit

Another great way to save freezer space and have almost-fresh fruit is to purchase large bags of frozen fruit to dehydrate. This is a sound way to store fruit that you cannot grow yourself. You will often find these bags on sale at the local grocery store.

There is no need to pretreat the fruit; the commercial packaging has already subjected the food to the blanching and oxidizing treatment. All you have to do is start with a bag of frozen fruit, spread it evenly onto your dehydrator trays, and set the heat to 125° to 130°F. Dry for six to eight hours. If you can get it set up before bed, they will be completely dry in the morning when you wake up.

Frozen fruit has a tendency to drip inside of the dehydrator as it dries, so if you are dehydrating more than one kind of fruit, it's best to place an extra Paraflexx sheet or plastic fruit leather tray under each type of fruit. That way, strawberry juice will not drip on the pineapple chunks below.

These fruits dehydrate well from a frozen state:

- Blueberries

- Mangoes

- Peaches

- Pineapple

- Strawberries

Buying Large Quantities of Produce

My food storage plan is based on bulk purchases. What that really means is that I look for items on sale and purchase them in quantity. I also wait until the right time to make those purchases.

Take fresh fruits and vegetables, for example. I know that blueberries are in season from June to August. I also know that when blueberries come to the grocery store or farmers market in June, they'll be expensive. Everyone wants fresh blueberries for their recipes, and the seller knows they can charge top dollar—and that we'll most likely pay—because they're fresh blueberries, after all!

By mid-August, the market will have been saturated, and fresh blueberries will not be such a hot off-the-shelf item. That's when the bulk purchaser gets their reward for waiting. The market will be flooded with berries that the farmers are trying to get out of their fields, and guess what—they will lower their prices to entice you to purchase. Now the price is so low that you can buy blueberries in bulk and preserve enough for the rest of the year. If you live near a blueberry farm and are willing to go to a u-pick event, you'll get an even better deal.

Don't overlook the local independent fruit stand businesses for making bulk purchases. They will often sell to you in bulk and give you a discount. Buying by the case or tray is usually cheaper anyway. You can also look at a big box store, like Costco or Sam's Club, or ask the local grocery store if they will sell to you at a discount if you purchase by the box.

There is always power in numbers, and bulk buying groups may be your answer. If you can join with other like-minded people to make your purchases together, you will get an even better deal. Here are some examples:

- Join a CSA and support a local farmer.

- Look for local food co-ops and see what they have to offer. These might be the best places to purchase dry goods like flour, grains, and beans. http://www.coopdirectory.org

- See if there is a Meetup group in your area that is purchasing in bulk. https://www.meetup.com

Still stumped? Create your own group. You must have like-minded friends! Do a Facebook poll and see which of your friends within a 20-mile radius are interested in saving money on their food storage. Once you have the basic group, brainstorm items that need to be purchased and put the group to work finding deals.

PURCHASE A BUSHEL, BAG, BOX, OR FLAT

Not all people have the time, space, or inclination for growing their own large garden and realistically, no one can grow everything that their family wants to eat. For example, bananas are hard to grow in most parts of the world. There is a whole grassroots movement around eating locally, but we will not delve into the benefits of it in this book. In most parts of the world, we are blessed to be able to purchase any fruit or vegetable from a local farmer, grocery, or big box store.

When I lived outside of Portland, Oregon, I would frequent a local produce stand called Justy's Produce and Flowers. I love that place and miss their helpful service and the ability to purchase fresh food in large quantities. So far, I have not found anything that compares here in Central Texas. I believe every town should have a helpful produce guy (or gal) that will find you a box of pickling cucumbers, or Roma tomatoes, at a terrific price. If you understand which produce is in season each month and the standard box size for purchasing in bulk, you, too, can save money and have enough to put into storage.

Packaging standards. Individual crops have specific industry packaging size and weight standards for sale in the wholesale market. This is done so everyone in the industry speaks that same packaging language, and everyone understands what they are buying and selling. Each crop has a different requirement for handling, so different size boxes, cartons, lugs, crates, flats, bags, sacks, and bulk bins are used as industry standards. Two common measurements are bushels and pecks. A bushel holds 8 gallons (32 quarts) of produce, which is equal to 4 pecks and 2,150 cubic inches. Here are some of the other common packaging standards that you should know.[4]

- *Bags* are paper and polyethylene, often with handles, and hold ¼ peck to ½ bushel

- *Baskets* are made of wood, and hold anywhere between ¼ peck and 1 bushel

- *Boxes, cartons, or hampers* hold anywhere from ½ peck to 1 bushel

- *Flats* hold 12 (1-pint) boxes

- *Lugs* are shallow containers, usually wood, that vary in size

- *Sacks* are 50 or 100 pounds of dry vegetables or commodities like potato, onion, beans, and rice

- *Trays* are used for berries and are made of corrugated paper. They hold either 6 to 8 quarts or 10 to 15 pounds

Grade and size standards. In addition, each produce crop is packaged in a uniform grade and size set by the U.S. Department of Agriculture or by individual states. Most of the fresh produce available for purchase in the grocery store is U.S. Grade No. 1 or better. The difference between No. 1 and lower grades is often small and has to do with how the

---

4 Karen Gast, "Containers and Packaging for Fruits and Vegetables," Postharvest Management of Commercial Horticultural Crops, March 1991, https://www.agmrc.org/media/cms/CD1_C07C95889B783.pdf.

product looks, not how it tastes. These products lower than No. 1, are often sold to institutions and companies who will turn them into a finished product.

I first learned about the grading system from Justy at his produce stand when I wanted a box of pickling cucumbers, and he asked me if U.S. No. 2 pickles were okay with me. He explained that they would be firm, fresh, and free from disease but irregular in diameter and color. Cucumber diameter and color are not important for my pickle making, so I went ahead and ordered. The price was significantly less.

The USDA publishes grade standards for each fruit[5] and vegetable[6] sold in the United States (visit the links in the footnotes to see the standards for individual fruit and vegetables). For example, apples are sold in five different grades:

- U.S. Extra Fancy

- U.S. Fancy

- U.S. No. 1

- U.S. No. 1 Hail

- U.S. Utility

Why do you, the home preserver, need to know these grade standards? Because you are also turning these apples into a finished product, and now that you know the language, you can purchase these lesser grades at a greatly reduced price. The difference between U.S. No. 1 and U.S. No. 1 Hail will not affect your applesauce in the slightest: "U.S. No. 1 Hail" consists of apples which meet the requirements of U.S. No. 1 grade except that hail marks where the skin has not been

---

5 United States Department of Agriculture, "Fruits," Agricultural Marketing Service, accessed November 13, 2017, https://www.ams.usda.gov/grades-standards/fruits.
6 United States Department of Agriculture, "Vegetables," Agricultural Marketing Service, accessed November 13, 2017, https://www.ams.usda.gov/grades-standards/vegetables.

broken and well-healed hail marks where the skin has been broken, are permitted, provided the apples are fairly well formed.[7]

You only need to ask your grocer or produce guy for these different grades. You can save significant money if you purchase this way.

7 United States Department of Agriculture, "Apple Grades & Standards," Agricultural Marketing Service, accessed November 13, 2017, https://www.ams.usda.gov/grades-standards/apple-grades-standards.

CHAPTER 5

STORING YOUR DEHYDRATED FOOD

The prepared pantry concept is at the core of my preparedness plan, and dehydrated foods play a big part. Once you've mastered drying your own food, you'll need to learn to store it properly so all your hard work will be edible for years to come.

Necessary Equipment

These basic supplies will keep dried food in a shelf-stable condition for a longer period of time. We use canning jars for most of our pantry storage. They are easy to find, easy to store, and can be used for all the food preservation processes you will be doing.

Storage containers naturally create a sealed environment for your food. To extend the shelf life, remove the oxygen from the storage container. This is done with oxygen absorbers. By removing the oxygen and creating a nitrogen environment, you will protect your food from insect damage and help preserve the quality. Oxygen-absorbing packets contain iron powder and work by reacting with the oxygen in your container, causing the powder to rust. They are not dangerous to your food.

You can purchase different sizes of oxygen absorbers depending on the container you are using for storage. You need one 100cc oxygen absorber per quart canning jar, and one 300cc oxygen absorber (or three 100cc absorbers) for each gallon of product. For storing 5- or 6-gallon buckets, you can purchase larger, 2000cc oxygen absorbers. You can find them at Discount Mylar Bags (http://www.discountmylarbags.com) or on Amazon.com.

You can also consider getting a vacuum sealer with a jar attachment. I use a FoodSaver vacuum sealer. These are handy to have and can be used instead of the 100cc oxygen absorbers when using canning jars. A vacuum sealer is helpful, but not necessary.

We use food-grade buckets for all of our long-term storage, including both edible and nonedible supplies. Look for plastic that has ⚠1 PETE or ⚠2 HDPE stamped on them. Find these at ULine.com, Wal-Mart, Amazon.com, or befriend a local bakery or ice cream shop.

Plastic freezer bags with zip tops are recommended for long- and short-term storage. They are sturdy and will keep out more air than regular storage bags.

Finally, plastic-coated foil Mylar pouches can be used instead of plastic freezer bags but this is the most expensive way to set up your storage. These sturdy bags are used in conjunction with oxygen absorbers to remove air and light from your dried food.

Short-Term Vs. Long-Term Pantry

We keep two types of pantry items in our house: short-term and long-term.

Short-term items. Our short-term pantry contains items that will be used in the next six months. Because these pantry items will have repeated exposure to light, heat, and humidity, they will have a shorter shelf life.

A short-term pantry might include bread and pancake mixes, along with other items with leavening; crackers; bars with dried fruit and nuts; quart-size containers of the most common dehydrated fruits and vegetables; and canned food and spices.

When we package our own food items, we store these small quantities in glass mason jars, food-grade plastic jars, or plastic zip-top bags. It's important to keep your short-term pantry clear of clutter, so you always know what is in there.

Linda Loosli at *Food Storage Moms* has a creative way to add extra space to a small pantry. She recommends that by taking the time to add "a few extra shelves to your small pantry, you gain almost 50 percent more cupboard space depending on how your cabinets are built." Her system also includes large and small buckets with flour and sugar for everyday baking, which she refills when needed. Find out more at https://www.foodstoragemoms.com/2013/10/small-pantry.

Long-term items. It is possible to keep home-processed food for two to five years if you remove the oxygen component. I do this by packaging dry food with a FoodSaver vacuum pack machine and placing these packages inside of plastic buckets with oxygen absorbers.

Here's the process. Once you have completely dried your fruits or vegetables and they have been properly conditioned (see page 30), it's time to package them for storage. Divide the food into smaller portion sizes (perhaps six meals) and package them using a FoodSaver Bag, which removes all the oxygen. If you don't have a FoodSaver, use 1-gallon zip-top freezer bags, remove as much air as you can, and add one 300cc oxygen absorber per gallon bag. If the item has sharp edges (like dried carrots), I also wrap it in a layer of plastic wrap to soften the edges. Be sure to label each of these smaller packages with the name of the product and the date it was dried, so you can rotate it properly.

Next, I place a 2000cc oxygen absorber in the bottom of a 5-gallon bucket and start layering in the smaller packaged items. You should be fairly quick about this. An oxygen absorber can only be exposed to air for 5 to 10 minutes before it begins to lose its potency. Once it's sealed, label the outside of the plastic bucket with the contents and the date it was sealed.

The smaller packages of items are stored in our extended pantry area and moved to the short-term pantry as needed. It is safe to open the 5-gallon buckets to remove packages, as long as the buckets are promptly re-sealed.

In addition to storing the food we dehydrate, we also purchase dehydrated vegetables, milk, and beans sealed in #10 cans from ProvidentLiving.org. Most dried food that is processed by professionals has a 20- to 30-year shelf life. At the time of this writing, a 2.4-pound can of diced onions was $9. It would take me almost 10 pounds of onions, untold hours, and I will have cried many tears to dry that many. The prices are very reasonable, so this is where I purchase my onions and carrots instead of drying them myself.

Keeping Inventory

It's hard to remember what you have on hand without an inventory system of some kind. It becomes even more difficult if you live in a small house and are storing items in nontraditional areas, like under beds or in closets. Keeping track of every item and where it's stored is essential, so you don't waste food.

This tracking system can be as simple as a yellow pad, an in-depth Excel spreadsheet, or even an online food storage tracker like Home Food Storage by Long Term Glass Wares, LLC.

I can honestly say that I have tried just about every inventory-keeping tactic on the market today and it's tough to keep my inventory list updated. The problem is that you have to get your family sold on keeping track of the food too, or they will remove food and mess up your system. Eventually, you may find that you will be the only person allowed to "check out" the food from the long-term areas in order to keep the inventory correct.

Rotating Your Food

Basic pantry protocols call for rotating your food. First-in-first-out (FIFO) is the best way to keep a rotation of fresh food. Rotating food FIFO means that each package of food has been dated, and you always have the oldest item stored at the front of the cabinet so you can use it first. When new items are added to storage, they are placed at the back of the cabinet.

There are several fancy ways to set up your shelves for FIFO storage, and making a rotating storage shelf may be the answer you are looking for. Search online for DIY building plans. Ultimately, the most important thing to remember when rotating food is to cook what you have in your pantry on a regular basis. If you are making soups, stews, and chili using dehydrated rather than fresh ingredients, you will always be using your current stock.

By labeling short-term and long-term storage containers with the contents inside and the date they were dried, you can keep track of your supply, rotate as needed, and avoid wasting the food that you put so much time and money into preparing.

CHAPTER 6

FRUIT AND VEGETABLE LEATHERS

Fruit leathers or fruit roll-ups are a favorite among kids and grownups alike. They are a wonderful way to use small quantities of fruit when they become too ripe for other drying methods. It's a treat that no one can pass up. You can use any kind of fruit that you have on hand. There are two basic preparation methods: uncooked and cooked fruit leather.

Sugar and honey are interchangeable in fruit leather recipes. Honey will produce a slightly tackier roll and a deeper flavor. Consider substituting pure maple syrup for a different taste. If you're using sugar, it's best to create simple syrup first, so you can be sure there are no granules in the finished product. Sugar will create a slightly more brittle finished product.

Dehydrator Trays Liners for Making Leather

A regular dehydrator tray is not going to trap the pureed food used in a fruit leather. Most commercial dehydrators come with one or two plastic fruit roll sheets specifically for this process. These are made from a rigid plastic with a slight outer lip that traps the food and keeps it from coming off the tray. Even if you purchased your machine used, it is easy to find additional trays online. If you make a lot of fruit leather, you may want to purchase enough liners to fit each tray.

Using a round machine is not the most efficient way to make leather, so I prefer to make mine in the square Excalibur machine. Their non-stick dehydrator sheets work terrifically for this, and they are easy to clean.

It's not necessary to go out and purchase something expensive as a liner for your leather; you can easily use parchment paper or plastic wrap and cut it to the size of your dehydrator trays. If you are going to be making leather on round trays, be sure to leave the middle section uncovered, as this is where the airflow takes place during the drying process. Foil and wax paper are not suitable for this project.

If you have trouble keeping your puree on the trays, create a bowl with your tray liners by pinching each corner together and securing them with 1-inch office binder clips.

General Instructions for Uncooked Fruit Leather

1. Thoroughly wash the fruit. If using nonorganic fruit, use the cleaning method found on page 35 to remove as much dirt and pesticide as possible.

2. Remove stones and large seeds. For fruit with small seeds, like strawberries, blackberries, and raspberries, seed removal is a personal preference. This is best accomplished by blending the berries into a pulp and then pushing the pulp through a fine mesh strainer. The pulp will flow through, and the seeds will be caught.

3. Peel the fruit and remove rough skins that are not usually eaten (melon, citrus). I tend to leave skins on my fruit if at all possible; there are many nutrients to be gained from leaving on the skin.

4. Cut the fruit into medium pieces and place them into a blender or food processor. Add citrus or ascorbic acid if you are worried about oxidation of the fruit (see page 28). Blend the fruit to a thick puree.

5. If the puree is too juicy, drain it through a fine mesh strainer until it has a thick pudding-like consistency. This is all a matter of preference, so don't be afraid to experiment. You will learn the consistency that is right for your machine and the fruit being used. If the batch is too thick, add water in 1-teaspoon increments until you reach the desired consistency.

6. Taste the mix and add honey or sugar, to taste. Add any spices at the quantity of ½ teaspoon per 4 cups of pureed fruit.

7. Prepare your drying trays and add the fruit puree to within an inch of the edge. Using a ladle, scoop and spread the puree evenly on the tray. It should be no more than ¼ inch thick or the drying time will be affected. The outside areas of the tray dry faster, so they should be thicker than the center. Swirl the puree around with a ladle to redistribute it the way you want.

8. Dry at 125°F for six to eight hours until the leather is sticky. Once it is dry, it will be translucent and slightly tacky to the touch. It will easily peel away from the plastic wrap or dehydrator sheet. It is best removed when warm.

General Instructions for Cooked Fruit Leather

Sometimes it is best to cook fruit before making a puree. Simmering the fruit before placing it in the dehydrator helps to cook down watery produce and concentrates the flavor. Some fruits, like rhubarb or cranberries, are always cooked before being eaten and would not taste good in a puree if you skipped this step. Other fruits, like apples, pears, coconuts, cherries, and blueberries, need to be softened before they will come to a smooth puree consistency.

1. Wash and prepare the fruit as described in steps 1, 2, and 3 starting on page 53.

2. Cook the fruit in a saucepan. Help the fruit break down as it cooks by mashing it with a fork.

3. Add honey or sugar, to taste, and ascorbic acid to prevent oxidization, if you'd like.

4. Blend the fruit to a thick puree.

5. Continue with steps 5 to 8 from the instructions above.

Get creative with your finished fruit leathers. They can be rolled and eaten as is, or rehydrated and used in pie fillings and dessert toppings. Make them into a beverage by combining five parts water with one part leather in a food blender.

How to Store Fruit Leather

Fruit leather is easiest to work with when it is still slightly warm. If you let it completely cool, take five minutes to warm it up in the dehydrator. After the leather is dry and there are no sticky parts, there are several ways to store it.

1. Lay a sheet of leather out on a piece of parchment paper or plastic wrap and roll it up like a scroll. Using kitchen shears, cut the scroll into 1-inch sections. If you want to create bite-size pieces, cut 1-inch squares from the sections. If you wish to skip the paper, it's still possible to roll the fruit leather, but it may need to be coated so it won't stick together. Dusting it with cornstarch or arrowroot powder is an option. Neither of these will change the flavor of the finished product.

2. Store your cut rolls in plastic freezer bags or a tightly sealed canning jar in a cool, dry place. For long-term storage, big batches can be stored in the freezer or refrigerator. We keep a batch in a jar in the pantry and include a 100cc oxygen absorber.

What Can Go Wrong

Properly dried fruit leather will be translucent and slightly tacky to the touch. It will easily peel away from the plastic wrap or dehydrator sheet. However, if the finished product is too brittle, there is a way to rehydrate it slightly.

1. Place the leather sheet back in the dehydrator on a tray.

2. Wet a paper or cloth towel and add it to a separate dehydrator tray.

3. Place the tray with the towel under the tray with the brittle sheet.

4. Place the cover on the machine and let the machine sit. Do not turn on the heat.

5. Check back after several hours or even overnight. The leather will have absorbed some of the moisture from the air.

6. If the finished product is too sticky, return the tray to the dehydrator and dry in 15-minute increments until the center is no longer sticky.

Vegetable Leather

Vegetable leathers are easy to make and can be used as veggie wraps when you roll them up with your favorite spreads. These leathers will keep for 6 to 12 months if stored in plastic bags or canning jars in the freezer. Break them up and make a powder, or stir bits into soups or casseroles.

Dry pureed, cooked vegetables on trays in the dehydrator at 135° to 140°F using the instructions below. The process is the same as for fruit leather, except you will always use the cooked method.

1. Select, wash, and prepare the vegetables in small pieces.

2. Cook the vegetables in a skillet or saucepan until soft.

3. Drain off any excess liquid.

4. Add spices, to taste.

5. Blend the mixture to a thick puree.

6. Prepare your drying trays and add the vegetable puree within an inch of edge. Using a ladle, scoop and spread the puree evenly on the tray. It should be no more than ¼ inch thick or the drying time will be affected. The outside areas of the tray dry faster, so they should be thicker than the center. Swirl the puree around with a ladle to redistribute it the way you want.

7. Dry at 135° to 140°F for 8 to 12 hours until the leather is finished. Once it is dry, it will be translucent and slightly tacky to the touch. It will easily peel away from the plastic wrap or dehydrator sheet. It is best removed when warm.

Vegetable leather can be used several ways:

• A savory, portable snack

• Paste for spaghetti sauce or pizza

• Reconstituted in soups

Highly Concentrated Food

Dehydrated fruit and vegetables lose between 80 percent and 90 percent of their moisture during drying. That makes the food highly concentrated, smaller, and lighter, so when you are eating it, the serving sizes can be deceiving. A cup of dehydrated apple chunks doesn't look like much, but it took two to three medium apples to make it. Would you really eat that many apples in one sitting? How about tomatoes—it takes nine medium tomatoes to make 1 cup of tomato dices!

If you are limiting the amount of sugar in your diet, a large portion of dried fruit will have concentrated fructose levels, potentially causing tooth decay in kids.

Finally, there's more fiber in dehydrated food, and while fiber is actually good for you in small doses, the high levels found in dried fruit could quickly lead to intestinal problems like gas, bloating, cramping, and diarrhea. It's best to be aware and take note of portion sizes, and extra calories, so you can adjust your snack sizes accordingly.

CHAPTER 7

MAKING JERKY

Once you've learned the art of making jerky, you have the ability to raise your food storage plan to a higher level. Not only are you producing fruit and vegetables, but now you're also making a protein that is all-natural and free of additives, food colorings, and preservatives.

Homemade jerky can be made from any lean meat. Choose beef round, flank and chuck steak, rump roast, and brisket. Most cuts of pork, venison, turkey, or chicken work well. Stay away from highly marbled and fatty cuts.

Safe Jerky

The temperature of raw meat while processing jerky is of particular concern. You must use a dehydrator that reaches a temperature of 160°F so it will kill harmful microorganisms that may be present on meat. If your dehydrator does not have a blowing fan and the ability to reach 160°F, it is not suitable for making homemade jerky.

Safe meat handling procedures should be followed at all times. Wash your hands with soap and water and use clean utensils. Never cross-contaminate different batches of meat by using the same cutting board, knife, or tongs.

Thaw meat in the refrigerator, never on the countertop. Leaving food out too long at room temperature can cause bacteria (such as *Staphylococcus aureus*, *Salmonella enteritidis*, *Escherichia coli O157:H7*, and *Campylobacter*) to grow to dangerous levels that can cause illness. Bacteria grow rapidly in the range of temperatures between 40°F and 140°F, doubling in number in as little as 20 minutes. This range of temperatures is often called the "Danger Zone."[8]

Prepare the Meat

First, remove any visible fat and connective tissue from the meat. Fat becomes rancid and quickly takes on an off flavor. Using a fatty meat will greatly reduce the shelf life of your finished product.

Meat is easier to cut when it is partially frozen, especially if you do not have an electric meat slicer. Cut it into strips no thicker than ¼ inch, 1 to 1½ inches wide, and 4 to 8 inches long. The bigger the piece of meat, the longer it will take to dry. For chewy jerky, cut with the grain of the meat; for brittle jerky, slice across the grain.

Pretreating the Meat

To reduce spoilage, you need to reduce the amount of bacteria on the meat. This can be done by using one of three methods to treat the meat before drying: presoaking in vinegar, marinating and precooking the meat, or freezing the meat before cooking. If the meat has been frozen for 60 days, all bacteria are destroyed and soaking or precooking is not necessary.

---

8 United States Department of Agriculture, "Danger Zone," USDA Food Safety and Inspection Service, June 28, 2017, https://www.fsis.usda.gov/wps/portal/fsis/topics/food-safety-education/get-answers/food-safety-fact-sheets/safe-food-handling/danger-zone-40-f-140-f/ct_index.

Vinegar presoak. Slice the meat, add it to a large bowl, cover with a 5 percent vinegar solution, and soak for 10 minutes. Drain the meat from the vinegar presoak and place it in a plastic zip-top bag to get ready for marinating.

Add any brine ingredients to the marinating bag, making sure that all pieces of meat are completely covered. Add additional water if necessary. Refrigerate one to four hours or overnight. Drain before dehydrating.

Marinate and precook. Slice the meat. Add the brine ingredients to the marinating bag, making sure that all pieces of meat are completely covered. Add additional water if necessary. Refrigerate one to four hours or overnight.

Precook the meat to reduce chances of food-borne illness. Add the strips of meat and marinating sauce to a large pot and boil, uncovered, for five minutes, or until the meat reaches an internal temperature of 160°F. Drain.

Dehydrating the Jerky

Place the strips in a single layer on dehydrator sheets, pat each piece dry with a paper towel so they are not dripping marinade, and make sure they don't touch or overlap. There is no need to rinse. Dehydrate at 160°F. After four hours, check the batch and remove any small pieces that are dry. Depending on slice size, the whole batch will take approximately four to six hours to complete. Remove dried strips from the trays and cool. Jerky is done when you can take a piece and bend it. It should crack and leave strands, but not break.

If the meat strips were not pretreated in marinade prior to drying, you might want to take an extra drying step in an oven after dehydrating. Place the dried strips on a baking sheet and cook at 275°F for 10 minutes, or until the jerky reaches an internal temperature of 160°F. Remove any visible fat beads before packaging for storage.

Creating Specialty Jerky Brines

There are many ideas online for creating jerky. Ultimately, flavorful brine sets the stage for your success. Once you learn the basics of making brine, you are free to experiment and create a one-of-a-kind creation that your family will love. Your specialty jerky brine needs at least three of these four elements: salt, acid, sweetness, and spice. Even a savory marinade benefits from a little sweetness, so most brine incorporates all four elements.

Salt helps to preserve and provides flavor. Try kosher salt, canning salt, sea salt, and table salt. Soy sauce is another option, but you should still add some traditional salt too.

Acids include apple cider vinegar, balsamic vinegar, lemon juice, lime juice, soy sauce, white vinegar, and wine.

Sweeteners are optional and include sugar, brown sugar, corn syrup, fruit juice, honey, and molasses.

Spices and seasonings are optional but encouraged, and include dill seed, garlic, mustard seed, onion, paprika, pepper, red pepper, and just about anything that you can think of.

Try some of these combinations, look at commercially prepared products for ideas, and try our favorite recipes from this book.

- Classic Beef (page 149)
- Beef Steak (page 150)
- Spicy Cajun (page 149)
- Teriyaki (page 149)
- Chile Lime
- Garlic Chili
- Hatch Chili and Onion
- Orange Chipotle
- Pineapple Orange

Storing Jerky

Jerky is not a long-term storage item. It can be stored in sealed bags at room temperature for up to two weeks. For the longest shelf life and flavor, homemade jerky can be stored in containers in the refrigerator for up to one month, or in the freezer for up to six months.

Rehydrating Jerky in Meals

We often think of jerky as a tasty snack for quick days or to take on hiking trips, but the meat can be rehydrated and successfully used in soup and stew. In a large saucepan, combine 3 cups water, 1 cup jerky chunks, and any dehydrated vegetables you will be using. They should be completely covered with the water. Suggested vegetables include tomato, potato, bell pepper, onion, carrot, or garlic. Add any additional water as the meat and vegetables expand, if needed. Allow the mix to sit for 30 minutes to rehydrate. Once rehydrated, place the pan over medium heat and bring to a boil. Add any fresh ingredients and spices, then simmer for an additional 30 minutes to an hour, until jerky is tender and fresh vegetables are cooked.

CHAPTER 8

SOUPS, POWDERS, AND HERBS

You may often find yourself with leftover fruit, vegetables, and herbs that could be put to good use. In this chapter we'll discuss the pros and cons of dehydrating soup, how to make your own specialized powders, and how to dry herbs for tea and crafts.

Soups

Similar to making fruit and vegetable leather, soup becomes a quick precooked meal that just needs hot water to bring it back to life. Unlike leather, soup is first cooked on the stove and dried until it is crisp. The vegetables must be cooked for this to be an instant meal. Otherwise, vegetables that were only blanched during processing will still be in their partially uncooked form. This technique works best with a thick soup recipe, like split pea, carrot, or winter squash, because they will stay on the trays instead of running off. Soup with a broth base is not a good choice.

IS IT WORTH IT?

That depends on the kind of meals you want to prepare. I tend to be the sort of cook that takes several dry ingredients from the pantry, drops them into a pot of bouillon, broth, or water, and makes a tasty meal from the things we have on hand. This method assumes that you have the time to cook from scratch at home. If you find that you need a homemade soup meal for busy days, traveling, or backpacking trips, a make-ahead soup might be just the thing. With one day of hard work and a bit of preplanning, you can make a large batch of healthy soup that is easily prepared, dried, and stored for when you need it. Store single serving portions in jars in a dark, cool pantry for up to six months.

TIPS FOR SUCCESS

1. This technique should only be used for soup without meat or dairy, and that has very little fat. Such ingredients will shorten the shelf life of the dry soup. Do not choose a recipe that uses milk as the base unless you are willing to cook with water and add powdered milk when packaging.

2. Thoroughly cook the ingredients of the soup on the stovetop to the desired thickness. Remember, the boiling water used during serving will not cook the food, only rehydrate it, so everything must be thoroughly cooked.

3. Consider using an immersion blender to get the vegetables into smaller, uniform pieces before drying.

4. Typically, one dehydrator tray of soup equals one serving. For quick drying, spread one or two ladles of soup on Paraflexx or plastic tray covers no more than ¼ inch thick.

5. Dry on dehydrator trays for four to eight hours until the soup is brittle. You may need to peel the soup off the tray and flip it halfway through the drying cycle.

6. Run one tray of dry soup through a blender until it reaches a powder consistency and measure it. This will help you know how much is required for one serving.

7. Determine the amount of boiling water needed to reconstitute one tray (one serving) of soup to the thickness you like. Typically, 1 to 1½ cups of water will do.

8. Package the soup in canning jars in single serving portions. Make sure there is enough space left in the jars to add the boiling water. These jars can handle the heat and will not break or melt.

9. Make a recipe card with the name of the soup and the directions to use when serving. Place it inside of each jar, listing the amount of water needed and any other ingredients that will complete the recipe.

Powders

Pulverized fruit powder can be bought commercially, but it can be hard to find and somewhat expensive—especially for the home cook. However, powdering your own fruit, vegetables, and spices is an economical way to add nutrients to your food storage on a budget.

To start, follow the dehydrating directions found in Chapter 9 for your favorite fruit or vegetable. Food should be dried until moisture-free so if you try to squeeze two pieces of produce together, they will not stick. To get the desired texture, it is best if you dry the fruits or vegetables in small pieces. Aim for the light texture of copy paper. If the produce still feels moist, continue drying in two-hour increments until it dries throughout.

The dried product needs to be conditioned for one week to remove any remaining moisture. Place the dried fruit into a plastic bag or canning jar, filling the container no more than three-fourths full. Let the fruit sit, or condition, and shake the bag or jar once every day or two.

Some dehydrated fruits are inherently sticky due to their sugar content, like raisins, figs, plums, and apricots. These should be dried in very small pieces if you wish to powder them. Even when you are using a well-dried batch of fruit, stickiness is simply an innate quality of fruit powder. If you find that the finished product clumps, add ½ to 1 teaspoon of arrowroot powder to the fruit before blending; this will help to even out the clumps.

You can process small batches of fruit or vegetables in a food processor, blender, or coffee grinder until they are powdered. This is a cumbersome process that may take several tries, but is worth it.

Once you reach the grind you are looking for, transfer the powder to an airtight container and store it at room temperature for three months or in the refrigerator for six months. Be aware, homemade fruit and vegetable powder is not a long-term storage item, so only process as much powder as you think you will need for the next few months and leave the dried produce whole until you need another batch.

Here are some tasty suggestions for using homemade fruit or vegetable powder in your daily meals:

- Add it to hot or cold cereal
- Add it to the batter of doughs for muffins, cakes, or quick bread. In any recipe, replace ½ cup flour with ½ cup fruit powder
- Add powder to smoothies. Make a fruit smoothie milkshake by adding ¼ cup fruit powder, 1 cup milk, 1 tablespoon honey, and ice cubes to a blender
- Use it when making homemade ice cream, frozen yogurt, or sorbet
- Add it to meringue as a flavor enhancer and coloring agent
- Add fruit powder to your fermented beverages for a zingy second ferment
- Use it as a spice rub for meats

- Use it in glazes and frosting

- Rehydrate it for a fruit puree, like applesauce, at a later date

See the Tomato Powder recipe on page 131 for a more detailed example.

Herbs

Herbs have been dried and used for home health and hearth for thousands of years, and they are a big part of any preparedness garden. You probably have all the usual suspects already in attendance: rosemary, chives, oregano, and mint, just to name a few.

Dried herbs can be used to make herbal tea blends for protection against seasonal colds and flu, and as an addition to your prepared pantry as you create your own rubs and spice blends for cooking. They have many self-reliant uses:

- candles

- cleaners

- flavored vinegar

- herb-flavored oils

- potpourri

- seasonings

- shampoo

- soap

- tea blends

You can dry herbs in small batches throughout the growing season as time allows. In the long run, it costs less to purchase individual plants and dehydrate your own than it does to purchase dried herbs from the store. Your plants will respond to regular cuttings by growing thicker.

Pruning keeps them compact and prevents plants from flowering and setting seed, so you can have several harvests.

Look for fragrant herbs with large leaves. Everyone has their favorites, but these 10 herbs are easy to grow and versatile for cooking, tea, and healing.

- basil
- bee balm
- chamomile
- ginger
- lemon balm
- lemon verbena
- mint
- plantain
- rosemary
- stevia

There are only a few rules for harvesting and drying herbs.

1. Pick flowers at the peak of freshness. New leaves at the tips will have the most concentrated flavor.

2. Harvest flowers and leaves on a sunny day, just before the flowers open. The leaves should be completely dry, so harvest during a dry, sunny day in the mid-morning, after the dew has evaporated, or in the evening before the dew forms.

3. Use scissors to cut off your harvest. Leave 4 to 6 inches of stem on the plant for later growth.

4. Once harvested, keep the picked herbs out of direct sunlight until you can begin the drying process. Consider bringing a basket with a towel to cover the cuttings while you harvest.

DRYING HERBS

Begin drying freshly cut herbs as soon as possible, before they begin to wilt. Remove any bruised or imperfect leaves and stems. Inspect the harvest for seeds and insects. Discard these to the compost pile.

To preserve the volatile oils in your herbs, try to rinse and handle the leaves as little as possible. Rinse the stems in cool water and gently shake off excess moisture, then pat dry with a towel. Remove leaves from the stems and run them through a salad spinner, if you have one. Another easy way to remove excess water is to use a large muslin towel as a spinner. Just place the wet leaves inside the large towel, gather the corners, and head outside to swing it around a few times. The water will exit as you spin the towel.

The point of this spinning is to get the leaves as dry as possible before you begin the dehydrating process, in order to keep drying time way down. If you are growing organic herbs, there is no need to wash your herbs unless they are very muddy or buggy.

Microwave drying. This method is only safe for herbs and is the fastest way to dry if you only have a small harvest each day. It is done in small batches of 1 or 2 cups at a time. Spread a clean cup of leaves in a single layer between two sheets of paper towels, and microwave in 30-second intervals. If you have an oven with the wattage of 1,000 or higher, special attention is needed to make sure the leaves and paper do not catch fire. Trust me; I know this from experience!

After 30 seconds, check the leaves, turn them over, and heat for another 30 seconds. Remove small leaves as they are finished and repeat the process in 30-second increments until the herbs are crackly dry. This will only take two or three minutes.

Hanging. Hanging herbs in the kitchen can add a homey touch, but this is not the most efficient way to dry your herbs. Leaving them exposed to the air and sunlight for an extended period of time means they will lose their flavor.

To prevent this, you should lay cut stems out and sort them by size. Bunch six to ten stalks together in bundles and fasten them tightly with a rubber band or twist tie. The rubber band will not come loose as the herbs dry. It's best to hang the bundles out of direct sunlight and in a room that will not get too much moisture but has good air circulation. Bathrooms are not a good place to do this.

If you must hang them to dry in the sun, it should be done on a day with little humidity. Place the herb bundles in a paper bag that has several holes cut for circulation. Attach the bag to a string or clothesline using clothespins. These bags must be brought inside at night, so dew does not affect them. Depending on the humidity in your home, the drying time will be one to three days.

Screen drying. The goal with screen drying is to allow air circulation all around the screen. Keep the drying screens elevated by placing blocks underneath. Drying screens should not be placed in direct sunlight while drying.

The herbs can touch each other on the screens because they will shrink as they dry. Screen drying is a slower process than the other methods. Due to lack of airflow, the drying process will take from two to four days.

Dehydrator drying. Drying herbs in a dehydrator can be quite easy. Wash as directed above, separate the leaves from the stems, and lay them out in a single layer up to ¼ inch thick. It's okay to have them touch; herbs will not stick together while they dry.

Herbs are dried at cooler temperatures than fruits and vegetables to help reduce the evaporation of the essential oils during the drying process. For the best results, dry in the 90° to 100°F range. Strong herb flavors, like garlic, ginger, and rosemary, should be dried separately from mild herbs that might pick up their flavors. Drying times range from two hours for leafy herbs to six hours for woody stems or roots.

STORING HERBS

As soon as you've dried your herbs to a stage where they can easily be powdered between your fingers, they are ready for storage. Remove the leaves from the stalks (if you didn't do it before) and keep the leaves whole. Crumbling the leaves releases the aromatic oils that you want for your teas, tonics, and lotions, so do not crush the leaves until you are ready to add them to recipes. To use the herbs, crush the leaves in your hands or powder them in a mortar and pestle or with a rolling pin, then measure as directed by your recipe. Use sparingly; you'll want about one third of the amount of dried herbs as you would use fresh herbs in your recipes.

Keep the leaves in airtight containers. Mason jars work well, but any reclaimed lidded glass container will fit the bill. Glass works best because metal and plastic can affect the flavor of some herbs and after a while, the flavor will transfer to the container. I saved chopped peppermint in a 1-gallon plastic jug. It's been in there for a few years. The herbs are still fragrant, but I will never be able to store anything else in the jar; the scent has completely permeated the container. From now on, it is peppermint or nothing!

The recommended storage time for herbs is one year. It is best practice to grow enough fresh herbs to last from harvest to harvest. After one year, the herbs will still be good, just not as aromatic. I use my older herbs for soaps and craft projects. No matter what, your herbs should be stored in a cool, dark place, away from heat.

If you have a bumper crop of your favorite herb, you can remove the oxygen from the jar and freeze herbs in FoodSaver containers. As long as you keep moisture out of a storage container, you can get up to 18 months of storage in the freezer.

CHAPTER 9

DEHYDRATING 50 COMMON FRUIT AND VEGETABLES

In this chapter, we'll take the guesswork out of dehydrating your favorite fruit and vegetables. You may even find food that you did not know you could dry for home storage. Each entry lists the best way to clean, cut, dry, and rehydrate individual items for future use in your prepared pantry.

Apples

Apples are first on the list and are possibly the easiest fruit to start dehydrating. Once you have them clean, they require only a little preparation. We like to leave the skin on our apples for extra fiber and nutrition. They make a healthy snack all on their own.

Clean: For nonorganic apples, follow the cleaning tips on page 35. Wash organic applies with warm water. Dry apples with a cloth.

How to prepare: Use an apple peeler/corer for consistently sized cuts. Otherwise, core and slice into eight equal-size pieces, or use a mandoline slicer.

Suggested thickness: ⅛ inch for chips; small chop for baking

Drying time: 6 to 12 hours, depending on thickness

Temperature: 125°F

Consistency when dry: Leathery to crisp, with no moisture in the middle

Blanching requirements: N/A

Oxidizing treatment: Treat cut pieces with ascorbic acid or lemon juice.

How to rehydrate: Pour boiling water over the dried apples until just covered and let pieces soak for 30 minutes, or until they rehydrate to the consistency you are looking for.

Consistency when rehydrated: Like cooked apples (soft)

Yield: 2 to 3 medium apples = 1 cup dried apples = 1¼ cups rehydrated apples

Apricots

Apricots are worth waiting for, even with their extended drying time. Use rehydrated in pies and other desserts, and dried as a healthy snack.

Clean: For nonorganic apricots, follow the cleaning tips on page 35. Wash organic apricots with warm water, then dry.

How to prepare: Remove pit. No need to remove skins.

Suggested thickness: Cut in half or in quarters for quicker drying time.

Drying time: 8 to 12 hours for quarters; 12 to 24 hours for halves.

Temperature: 125°F

Consistency when dry: Leathery

Blanching requirements: N/A

Oxidizing treatment: Use lemon juice or ascorbic acid, if you want them to retain their light color.

How to rehydrate: Soak in hot water or warmed juice for 15 to 20 minutes, or simmer on the stovetop, until the fruit is plump and has absorbed the water.

Consistency when rehydrated: Soft and plump

Yield: 2 pounds fresh apricots = 6 ounces dried apricots = 2 cups rehydrated apricots

Asparagus

Asparagus is a beloved vegetable at our house, and we can eat it every day for weeks. The growing season is short, and when asparagus is out of season, it is expensive. In order to save money on our favorite veggie and keep it on the table, we dehydrate it as much as possible. Process dried pieces into powder and add it to soup.

Clean: For nonorganic asparagus, follow the cleaning tips on page 35. For organic asparagus, wash with warm water and pat dry well.

How to prepare: Cut off tough ends first.

Suggested thickness: 1-inch pieces

Drying time: 8 to 12 hours

Temperature: 125°F

Consistency when dry: Brittle

Blanching requirements: Three to four minutes

Oxidizing treatment: N/A

How to rehydrate: Cover 1 cup asparagus with 2¼ cups of boiling water and soak for 30 minutes, or add dried pieces directly to soup.

Consistency when rehydrated: Soft, like cooked

Yield: 2 cups fresh asparagus = 1 cup dried asparagus = 1½ cups rehydrated asparagus

---

If you sort your cut asparagus pieces onto dehydrator trays by thickness, you will save time and additional work. The spear tips dry quite a bit faster than the fibrous stalks, so keeping them on separate trays saves you the time and effort of fishing them out from many pieces that have not finished drying.

Bananas

Achieving the texture of store-bought banana chips is almost impossible for the home food processor that does not want unnecessary additives on their fruit. Did you know that in order to achieve that extra sweetness and crispness, they actually dip the bananas in sugar syrup and deep fry it? I'm assuming that you want to get away from the extra additives and calories as you are dehydrating fresh bananas for your food storage.

Used rehydrated banana in smoothies and in cereals, or chill the pieces and serve them on their own. Or, just enjoy as chips!

Clean: Wash and dry, then peel. There is no special treatment for organic versus nonorganic.

How to prepare: The best tasting bananas are slightly green at the top and have a few brown spots on the peel. Use overripe bananas in leather.

Suggested thickness: ⅛-inch rounds for chips

Drying time: 8 to 12 hours

Temperature: 125°F

Consistency when dry: Brittle, snaps easily

Blanching requirements: N/A

Oxidizing treatment: Dip or spray with lemon juice to prevent browning.

How to rehydrate: Mix one part water to one part chips, then simmer at a low temperature for five minutes.

Consistency when rehydrated: Like fresh

Yield: 5 large bananas = 2 cups dried bananas = 4 cups rehydrated bananas

---

Save the peels and dehydrate them too. They are a terrific potassium boost for your garden. Get instructions at http://preparednessmama.com/dry-banana-peels.

Beans (Green, Yellow, Snap)

If you are looking for a pantry-stable vegetable that is easy to dry and good for you, the green bean is it. While we do like to eat fresh beans from the garden, I prefer to purchase beans in large frozen bags from the grocery store to use for dehydrating. This is because I do not enjoy the process of cutting and blanching that is required for fresh beans. Thankfully, the local store has an excellent selection of organic beans, so my processing time is reduced to practically nothing. The peak season for green beans is from April to October, and you will get about 3 cups of beans per pound.

Clean: For nonorganic beans, follow the cleaning tips on page 35. For organic beans, wash with warm water and pat dry.

How to prepare: Remove strings if necessary. Cut before blanching. You do not need to prepare if dehydrating from the frozen state.

Suggested thickness: 1½-inch pieces, or cut lengthwise into 4-inch-long thin strips

Drying time: 8 to 14 hours

Temperature: 125°F

Consistency when dry: Hard, brittle

Blanching requirements: Boil or steam blanch for two to three minutes.

Oxidizing treatment: N/A

How to rehydrate: Cover 1 cup green beans in 2¼ cups warm water and soak for 30 minutes until plump. Or, add directly to soup without rehydrating.

Consistency when rehydrated: Like fresh

Yield: 2 cups fresh beans = 1 cup dried beans = 2 cups rehydrated beans

Beets

Harvest beets for storage late in the fall before the ground freezes. They have the best flavor when they are 2 inches in diameter. Except for gold varieties, beets will "bleed" away their color when cut.

Clean: For organic and nonorganic beets, scrub clean with a vegetable brush and warm water.

How to prepare: Cover with water and cook in a large saucepan until tender, about 45 minutes. Place the pot under running cold water and rinse until beets can be handled.

Suggested thickness: Peel, then cut into ⅛-inch strips.

Drying time: 8 to 12 hours; stir at four-hour mark.

Temperature: 125°F

Consistency when dry: Hard

Blanching requirements: N/A

Oxidizing treatment: N/A

How to rehydrate: Cover 1 cup dry beets in 2¾ cups warm water for one and a half hours.

Consistency when rehydrated: Like cooked

Yield: 2 cups fresh beets = 1 cup dried beets = 1½ cups rehydrated beets

---

Add 2 tablespoons of lemon juice or vinegar to the cooking water. This will help to keep the beets from bleeding.

Blueberries

If you are lucky enough to be able to grow blueberries in your own home garden, you're in for a treat. Dehydrated blueberries are fairly easy to make and will keep for over a year if stored properly in a cool, dry part of your pantry. Skip the processing time and use frozen berries.

Just as with processing cranberries (page 29), the outer shell of the blueberry needs to be pierced to make sure the heat reaches the inside and allows the berry to dry completely. This is accomplished by piercing each berry individually, which is time-consuming, or adding them whole to a metal strainer and submerging in boiling water for 30 seconds. If using frozen berries, it is not necessary to do the additional water bath processing or piercing.

Add rehydrated blueberries to muffins and pancakes or use the recipe on page 123 to make Blueberry Basil Syrup.

Clean: For nonorganic blueberries, follow the cleaning tips on page 35. Rinse delicately. Rinse organic berries with warm water and dry delicately.

How to prepare: Remove stems. Pierce each berry with a skewer or pin, blanch for 30 seconds, or freeze until solid.

Suggested thickness: Leave whole

Drying time: 10 to 18 hours

Temperature: 125 to 135°F

Consistency when dry: Hard, will not stick together when squeezed

Blanching requirements: See notes above.

Oxidizing treatment: N/A

How to rehydrate: Submerge in cool water for 10 to 15 minutes.

Consistency when rehydrated: Not as plump or juicy as fresh. In baked goods, use without rehydrating to keep moisture content down.

Yield: 2 pints fresh blueberries = 1 cup dried blueberries = 2 cups rehydrated blueberries

---

Berries will drip during dehydrating. Add an extra tray with a fruit leather insert below them to catch the juice and protect other items from getting juiced.

Broccoli

Broccoli is wonderful to have in the pantry. I like to powder broccoli stalks to use when making broccoli soup. Dried florets can be rehydrated for soup, stew, or even for cooking as a side dish. Look for a head with deep color and closed flowers.

Clean: For nonorganic broccoli, follow the cleaning tips on page 35. For organic broccoli, wash with warm water and pat dry.

How to prepare: Cut the head from the stalk. Separate the florets into equal-size pieces. Chop the stalk into equal-size chunks.

Suggested thickness: Equal-size pieces

Drying time: 8 to 12 hours; stalks may take longer.

Temperature: 125° F

Consistency when dry: Crisp

Blanching requirements: For florets, water blanch for two minutes or steam blanch for three minutes. For stalks, cook in boiling water for five minutes until tender, then drain.

Oxidizing treatment: N/A

How to rehydrate: Soak 1 cup broccoli in 2 cups water. Soak until liquid stops absorbing, for 30 to 60 minutes. There's no need to soak if you're adding the broccoli to a recipe that has water and requires cooking.

Consistency when rehydrated: Tastes fresh, although not crunchy

Yield: 2 cups fresh broccoli = 1 cup dried broccoli = 2 cups rehydrated broccoli.

Cabbage and Brussels Sprouts

Cabbage may not be the first vegetable on your dehydrating list, but it should be right up in the top 10. Its nutritional advantages make it a recommended addition to your pantry. The peak season for cabbage falls between October and January, and for each pound of cabbage, you can process 6 cups of freshly shredded leaves. When fresh, a tightly wrapped head will last 14 days in the refrigerator, but if you take the time to dehydrate, you can have "like fresh" leaves for an entire year. This process works for all varieties of cabbage, and it's not even smelly as it dries! To try your dried cabbage in a recipe, check out Slow Cooker Stuffed Cabbage Rolls on page 155.

Clean: For nonorganic cabbage, follow the cleaning tips on page 35. For organic cabbage, wash with cool water, and pat dry.

How to prepare: Remove the outer leaves and stem, and core the head. Slice into thin strips.

Suggested thickness: ⅛-inch shreds or whole leaves

Drying time: 8 to 12 hours

Temperature: 125° F

Consistency when dry: Flexible and dry, like paper

Blanching requirements: N/A

Oxidizing treatment: N/A

How to rehydrate: Soak one part dried cabbage in three parts cool water for three minutes, or add pieces directly to soup.

Consistency when rehydrated: Like fresh, but not as crisp

Yield: 3 cups fresh cabbage = 1 cup dried cabbage = 3 cups rehydrated cabbage

---

Some people swear by blanching cabbage and others don't think it's necessary at all. Try dehydrating your cabbage both ways and see which you prefer. Me? I'll skip the extra step every time! However, you can dehydrate whole cabbage leaves for use in a poultice for healing. To make a poultice, rehydrate the leaves in cool water and lay them flat between two sheets of plastic wrap. Use a rolling pin to bruise them; it gets the healing juice flowing. Next, place the leaves directly on your skin, cover with plastic wrap, and secure with a cloth wrap overnight.

Carrots

Carrots are a staple in my pantry. We use them several times a week in stir-fry meals and soups. They lose over 80 percent of their water during the dehydrating process and will shrink down to practically nothing when they are dry. Take this into account and use tray inserts when you are drying them, or you may find that they have fallen through to the bottom of your dehydrator.

Clean: For nonorganic carrots, follow the cleaning tips on page 35 and scrub with a vegetable brush. For organic carrots, place in a colander and scrub with a vegetable brush and warm water. No need to peel.

How to prepare: Slice off the top and bottom ⅛ inch, slice into rounds or cubes.

Suggested thickness: ⅛-inch rounds; ¼-inch cubes; shredded

Drying time: 10 to 12 hours

Temperature: 125°F

Consistency when dry: Hard, brittle

Blanching requirements: Blanch for three to four minutes in boiling water, until they are bright orange.

Oxidizing treatment: N/A

How to rehydrate: To get a like-raw texture, soak in cool water for 15 to 30 minutes. For cooked carrots, combine carrots and water in a one to one ratio, bring to a boil, cover, and reduce heat to low for 10 minutes. Add directly to soup or stew without rehydrating.

Be sure to add extra water to your recipe if you are adding carrots directly from a dehydrated state. They will take up a lot of liquid as they plump back to their original shape.

Consistency when rehydrated: Anywhere from crunchy to just-cooked, depending on rehydrating method

Yield: 2 cups fresh carrots = 1 cup dried carrots = 1¼ cups rehydrated carrots

Cauliflower

There are many ways to use cauliflower besides as a side dish. We puree it and use it as a thickener in soup and stew. If you grate it into small pieces (ricing), you can rehydrate and use it to make pizza crust or a mashed potato substitute. Try Cauliflower Soup (page 151) or Riced Cauliflower Pizza Crust (page 160).

The peak season for cauliflower is September to November, and the average size of a head is 2 pounds. Each pound of fresh cauliflower will lose 75 percent of its water and become ¼ pound when dried, so dehydrating is a nice way to extend the shelf life of this healthy vegetable.

Clean: Wash organic and nonorganic cauliflower with warm water and dry. If the heads are fresh from the garden, soak in salt water for 10 minutes to dislodge any bugs.

How to prepare: Remove large stalks and outer leaves.

Suggested thickness: Cut into small, 1- to 2-inch, uniform-size florets, or rice the cauliflower and set it to dry on fruit leather trays.

Drying time: 8 to 12 hours

Temperature: 125° F

Consistency when dry: Crisp

Blanching requirements: To keep the florets white, steam four to five minutes. Skip this step if you will be using it as an ingredient and the color isn't important. Cook large stalks until soft, cut, and add to trays.

Oxidizing treatment: N/A

How to rehydrate: Soak 1 cup cauliflower in 1 cup water for 15 to 20 minutes.

Consistency when rehydrated: Like cooked

Yield: 4 cups fresh cauliflower = 1 cup dried cauliflower = 4 cups rehydrated cauliflower

Celery

Celery is such a versatile vegetable, but most people rarely use the whole stalk before it goes bad. We dehydrate ours, so there is always a supply on hand for soup and stew. Don't forget to grind it and make celery salt for adding a savory flavor to salads and spice blends.

One head of celery fills two trays of my Nesco Gardenmaster dehydrator. The pieces will dry to half their size, so consider adding a catch tray so the smaller pieces won't slip through.

Clean: For nonorganic celery, follow the cleaning tips on page 35. For organic celery, wash with warm water and pat dry.

How to prepare: Cut off the ends and separate the stalks. If you are making celery powder, keep the leaves.

Place celery leaves and small pieces on a separate tray from the larger stalks. These will dry in half the time, and you won't have to fish them out from the rest of the batch.

Suggested thickness: ½-inch chunks

Drying time: Four hours for leaves; 8 to 12 hours for stalk pieces

Temperature: 125°F

Consistency when dry: Crisp

Blanching requirements: Steam for one minute if planning to rehydrate into whole pieces. Skip if you're planning to make powder.

Oxidizing treatment: N/A

How to rehydrate: Place whole pieces in warm water for 10 to 15 minutes, or add directly to soup or stew.

Consistency when rehydrated: Soft, like cooked

Yield: 3 cups fresh celery = 1 cup dried celery = 2 cups rehydrated celery

Cherries

Some people prefer to dip their cherries in boiling water for 30 seconds before they dehydrate them. I find that it is an unnecessary step that does not improve the quality of the dried fruit. However, if you are using a lighter cherry like Rainier or Emperor Francis, you may want to use an oxidizing treatment to preserve the color of the dried fruit.

Clean: For nonorganic cherries, follow the cleaning tips on page 35. Wash organic cherries with warm water, then dry.

How to prepare: Stem the fruit, cut in half, and remove the pit.

Use a skewer and water bottles as a cherry pitter.

Suggested thickness: Whole or half

Drying time: 12 to 24 hours

Temperature: 125° F

Consistency when dry: Should not stick together; dried cherry will click when dropped on a countertop.

Blanching requirements: Your preference

Oxidizing treatment: Your preference

How to rehydrate: Simmer on stovetop until rehydrated. Use in desserts and syrup.

Consistency when rehydrated: Chewy

Yield: 10 ounces fresh cherries = 1 cup dried cherries = 1½ cups rehydrated cherries

Citrus

Purchase thin-skinned citrus for the best flavor and juice. The peels can be used whole or made into powder for various recipes. Dried pieces can be steeped in vinegar to aid in cleaning, added to water for a tasty drink, or made into candied rinds. The pith can be used to make natural pectin. Powder the dried peels and mix with sugar, make lemon pepper spice, or add to scones and baked goods. Use in place of extract or zest.

All store-bought citrus must be washed to remove the wax coating before dehydrating.

Clean: For nonorganic citrus fruits, follow the cleaning tips on page 35. For organic fruits, wash with warm water then dry.

How to prepare: Use a mandoline for even cuts. Save the ends to dry for use in vinegar-based cleaner. Remove the pith and cut into strips.

Suggested thickness: ⅛-inch sliced rounds

Drying time: Four to eight hours

Temperature: 125°F

Consistency when dry: Crisp

Blanching requirements: N/A

Oxidizing treatment: N/A

How to rehydrate: Cover with cool water for 10 to 15 minutes.

Consistency when rehydrated: Like fresh

Yield: 1 medium orange or 2 to 3 lemons = 1 cup dehydrated citrus rounds = 1 tablespoon citrus powder = ¾ cup rehydrated citrus rounds

---

Dry the citrus ends with the rest of the batch and save them for making infused vinegar for cleaning. To use, add dried citrus ends to a canning jar and cover with white vinegar. Allow the mixture to steep for one to two weeks. Strain the citrus peels and discard to the compost pile. The vinegar can be diluted one to one with water and will retain the fresh scent.

Coconut

We don't often think about drying our own coconut, but if it is available in the grocery store, you should give it a try. The fresh taste of your own dried coconut is worth the effort. It also makes healthy milk for drinking and flour for baking. For ideas on how to use your dehydrated coconut, see Shredded Coconut (page 136), Coconut Flour (page 137), and Sweet Potato Coconut Flour Pancakes (page 154).

Clean: Wash and dry, then process using instructions below. There is no special treatment for organic versus nonorganic.

How to prepare: Poke a hole in the top of the nut and drain the water. Cut in half. Remove the outer bark and skin and shred or slice the meat into equal-size pieces.

Suggested thickness: Shredded, or cut into ⅜-inch pieces

Drying time: Four to eight hours

Temperature: 125° F

Consistency when dry: Leathery to crisp

Blanching requirements: N/A

Oxidizing treatment: N/A

How to rehydrate: Add twice as much hot water as coconut and soak for 30 minutes.

Consistency when rehydrated: Like fresh

Yield: 1 small coconut = 1 cup dehydrated coconut = 1½ cups coconut flour = ¾ cup rehydrated coconut

Corn

We eat a lot of corn but do not grow it ourselves because of where we live. Central Texas is corn country, and there are acres and acres of GMO corn growing in the field right next door. Corn is a wind-pollinated crop, and it is likely that there would be cross-pollination between the GMO corn and the open pollinated crops I would be growing. Instead, I purchase frozen organic corn in big bags from Costco. This saves us a ton of prep time, because there is no cutting or blanching required.

Clean: For nonorganic corn, follow the cleaning tips on page 35. For organic corn, wash with warm water and pat dry. No need to clean if using frozen corn.

How to prepare: Shuck the ears and clean each corn cob, removing all tassels. Place whole cobs in boiling water and cook until tender, six to eight minutes. Transfer to a bowl of ice water and allow the corn to cool. Use a de-cobber or sharp knife to remove the kernels from the cob. Pour kernels evenly onto dehydrator trays.

Suggested thickness: Individual kernels

Drying time: Six to eight hours for fresh; 8 to 10 hours for frozen

Temperature: 125° F

Consistency when dry: Brittle

Blanching requirements: See above.

Oxidizing treatment: N/A

How to rehydrate: Soak 1 cup corn in 2¼ cups water for half an hour. Or, add directly to soup, stew, and skillet meals.

Consistency when rehydrated: Like fresh cooked

Yield: 2 cups fresh corn kernels = 1 cup dried corn kernels = 1½ cups rehydrated corn

Cucumbers

While we often think of making pickles when we want to preserve cucumbers, putting them into the dehydrator can bring another dimension to your soups and sauces. You can take dried cucumber chips, process them into a powder, and add them to homemade salad dressing (see Creamy Cucumber Salad Dressing on page 130). Or you can include them in morning smoothies, or spice the chips up using the recipe for Zucchini Chips on page 146.

Clean: For nonorganic cucumbers, follow the cleaning tips on page 35. For organic cucumbers, wash with warm water, then dry.

How to prepare: Slice into rounds.

Suggested thickness: ¼ inch thick

Drying time: Four to six hours

Temperature: 135° F

Consistency when dry: Brittle; should snap when bent.

Blanching requirements: N/A

Oxidizing treatment: N/A

How to rehydrate: Soak in cool water for 30 to 60 minutes.

Consistency when rehydrated: Fresh tasting, limp texture

Yield: 1 cup fresh cucumber = ¼ cup dehydrated cucumber = ¾ cup rehydrated cucumber

---

You can make a pickle brine to rehydrate your cucumber slices. (See the Dehydrated Refrigerator Pickles recipe on page 148.) They'll turn out just as crunchy as fresh homemade refrigerator pickles. Or, you can dehydrate a jar of store-bought pickle spears or chips. Your family will love the change in texture, and it beats carrying a messy pickle in your lunch box. Be cautious though: These pickle chips are very salty when finished, and it is easy to eat a whole jar in one sitting.

Eggplant

Useful for Italian eggplant and tomato casseroles, eggplant will darken if not blanched before processing for storage. Oriental eggplant is long and thin and has a milder flavor than standard grocery store eggplant. It makes an excellent garden crop for USDA Plant Hardiness Zones 4 to 11.

Clean: For nonorganic eggplant, follow the cleaning tips on page 35. For organic eggplant, wash with warm water and pat dry.

How to prepare: Dice, slice, or cube. Prepare as you would use in recipes.

Suggested thickness: ¼ inch thick

Drying time: 6 to 12 hours

Temperature: 125°F

Consistency when dry: Leathery

Blanching requirements: Blanch for 15 seconds in boiling water.

Oxidizing treatment: N/A

How to rehydrate: Combine eggplant and cool water in even ratio, and then soak for 30 minutes.

Consistency when rehydrated: A bit leathery, but the flavor is excellent, like cooked eggplant.

Yield: 2 cups fresh eggplant = 1 cup dried eggplant = 1¼ cups rehydrated eggplant

Figs

Figs are extremely sticky as they dry. Be sure that they do not overlap or they will stick together. Consider using parchment paper on the trays for easy cleanup. Be sure to use only ripe fruit for this project. Before storage, lightly toss your figs with sugar if they stick together.

For any recipe calling for peaches, pears, prunes, or dates, you can successfully substitute figs. Try out these fruits by making Oatmeal Fig Cookies on page 176.

Clean: For nonorganic figs, follow the cleaning tips on page 35. Wash organic figs with warm water and pat dry.

How to prepare: For fresh figs, remove stems and cut out blemishes. Pierce the skin if drying whole small figs.

Suggested thickness: Cut in half or quarter. Place figs on the tray skin-side down.

Drying time: Time varies. Start checking at eight hours; could take up to 24 hours to finish. Turning the fruit may speed up the process.

Temperature: 125° F

Consistency when dry: Leathery and flexible

Blanching requirements: If drying figs whole, plunge in boiling water for 30 seconds.

Oxidizing treatment: N/A

How to rehydrate: Pour enough boiling water to cover, then let sit for 30 minutes.

Consistency when rehydrated: Not typically rehydrated. Used dried as snacks and in recipes.

Yield: 2 cups fresh fig pieces = 1 cup dried figs

Extend the shelf life of store-purchased dried figs by running them through the dehydrator for a few hours.

Garlic

Garlic seasoning is a pantry staple at our home; we use it with almost every meal. Garlic is planted in the fall after the first frost, and there are over 50 different varieties of soft-neck and hard-neck garlic adapted to every growing region. If possible, try to grow your own garlic and preserve it; the fresh taste will be worth it. You can purchase garlic cloves for planting at TheGarlicStore.com, SeedSavers.org, or TerritorialSeed.com. Using the square-foot gardening spacing method, you can grow nine cloves per square foot.

If you are not the gardening type, purchase large jars of organic garlic from a big box store and save yourself a lot of chopping time. A 32-ounce container will run you around $14 and make approximately 8 ounces of garlic powder when it's dried.

Clean: For organic and nonorganic garlic, separate and peel cloves, then remove root ends.

How to prepare: Slice with a mandoline or chop in a food processor.

Suggested thickness: See above.

Drying time: 6 to 12 hours

Temperature: 125° F

Consistency when dry: Crisp

Blanching requirements: N/A

Oxidizing treatment: N/A

How to rehydrate: Use as powder or break into bits for soup or stir fry.

Consistency when rehydrated: Like cooked

Yield: 1 cup fresh garlic = ¼ cup dehydrated garlic = ¾ cup rehydrated garlic

---

Store the dried garlic in an airtight container in the freezer and grind it as you are using it in recipes. It will keep its freshness for over a year if stored this way.

Ginger

Candied ginger is expensive, so we make our own. The cooking process also makes ginger syrup, which can be bottled and used for ginger ale, on pancakes, or drizzled over your favorite oatmeal. See page 174 for our Candied Ginger recipe!

Clean: For organic and nonorganic ginger, wash with warm water and dry.

How to prepare: Peel if making candied ginger.

Suggested thickness: ⅛-inch slices

Drying time: Four to six hours

Temperature: 135° F

Consistency when dry: Pliable

Blanching requirements: No need to cook if chopping for ground ginger. If making candied ginger, see instructions on page 174.

Oxidizing treatment: N/A

How to rehydrate: Not usually rehydrated. Instead, chop and use in salads, cookies, gingerbread, or in herbal tea.

Consistency when rehydrated: N/A

Yield: 1 cup fresh ginger = ½ cup dried ginger = ¾ cup rehydrated ginger

Grapes

If you are lucky enough to grow your own grapes, you have an advantage. Commercially grown grapes are notorious for pesticide residue and are consistently in the top 10 of the Environmental Working Group (EWG) list of "Dirty Dozen"[9]. Pay special attention to cleaning your nonorganic grapes before dehydrating.

Clean: For nonorganic grapes, follow the cleaning tips on page 35. Wash organic grapes with warm water, then dry.

How to prepare: Remove from stems after blanching.

Suggested thickness: Leave whole

Drying time: 15 to 30 hours, depending on size

Temperature: 135° F

Consistency when dry: Pliable

Blanching requirements: Dip in boiling water for 30 seconds, then into ice water to cool. This makes the skins ready for processing and reduces the drying time by half.

9 "DIRTY DOZEN: EWG's 2017 Shopper's Guide to Pesticides in Produce," EWG, Accessed November 13, 2017, https://www.ewg.org/foodnews/dirty_dozen_list.php#. We5VcGiPKUk.

Oxidizing treatment: N/A

How to rehydrate: N/A

Consistency when rehydrated: Dried grapes are raisins and cannot be reconstituted. Use dried in recipes or for snacks.

Yield: 1 cup fresh grapes = ¼ cup raisins

Dried and powdered grape leaves make a nice tea. Wash the leaves and pat dry. Pile the grapes on dehydrator trays, no more than ½ inch thick, then stir after three hours. Dry at 90°F for approximately six hours, or until crisp.

Green Onions and Leeks

Green onions and leeks dehydrate extremely well with minimal effort. Look for them to go on sale during their peak season, August to December, and stock up.

Clean: Prepare organic and nonorganic onions by washing with cool water, and pat to dry.

How to prepare: Cut off root ends, cut off ¼ inch from tops, remove any limp leaves.

Suggested thickness: Slice into ½-inch-thick rings.

Drying time: 8 to 12 hours

Temperature: 125°F

Consistency when dry: Papery

Blanching requirements: N/A

Oxidizing treatment: N/A

How to rehydrate: Add directly to soup, or spritz with cool water.

Consistency when rehydrated: Like fresh

Yield: 2 cups fresh green onions = 1 cup dried green onions = 1¼ cups rehydrated green onions

---

Separate green stalks from white ends on dehydrator trays. The tops will dry at a different rate, and this will keep you from picking out the dried parts while waiting for the rest to finish.

Horseradish

Horseradish is an old-fashioned crop enjoying a comeback in the garden. Harvest the roots each fall and leave enough roots in the ground for next year's crop. Make your own sauce in a blender with ¼ cup grated root, 1 tablespoon mustard, 1 teaspoon vinegar, 1 cup sour cream, and salt and pepper to taste.

Clean: Wash organic and nonorganic horseradish with warm water and a vegetable brush, then dry.

How to prepare: Remove small rootlets and stubs. Peel and scrape the root.

Suggested thickness: Grate and spread in a single thickness on dehydrator trays.

Drying time: Four to eight hours

Temperature: 125° F

Consistency when dry: Brittle

Blanching requirements: N/A

Oxidizing treatment: N/A

How to rehydrate: Soak 1 cup horseradish in 1 cup warm water for 30 minutes; rehydrating not necessary if using horseradish in cooking.

Consistency when rehydrated: Like fresh

Yield: 1 cup fresh horseradish = ½ cup dehydrated horseradish = ¾ cup rehydrated horseradish

---

Store the horseradish pieces in a vacuum-sealed jar until you need to use it. Break off a piece and run it through a coffee grinder that you set aside just for pungent herbs and spices.

Kale

Kale is enjoying a health food craze right now. It is high in iron, vitamin K, and vitamin A, and is filled with powerful antioxidants. Dehydrate with the purpose of making powder for smoothies (see powdering instructions on page 66), or experiment with making your own seasoned Kale Chips (page 145).

Clean: For nonorganic kale, follow the cleaning tips on page 35. For organic kale, wash with cool water and pat dry.

How to prepare: Discard the stems by pinching or slicing.

Suggested thickness: 2- to 3-inch-wide pieces

Drying time: Two to six hours

Temperature: 135° F

Consistency when dry: Crisp and papery

Blanching requirements: N/A

Oxidizing treatment: N/A

How to rehydrate: Use in smoothies or soup, eat dry as a chip.

Consistency when rehydrated: Like cooked

Yield: 2 cups fresh kale = 1 cup dried kale = 2 cups rehydrated kale

Kiwi

Kiwi grows on a vine in fairly acidic soil and can grow prolifically if you have the right conditions. It needs one male plant for every eight female plants, sturdy support, and temperatures with at least 240 frost-free days. Dried kiwi is best used as snacks and in a fresh salad.

Clean: Wash organic and nonorganic kiwi with warm water, then dry.

How to prepare: Remove peel.

Suggested thickness: Cut into ⅜- to ½-inch slices. Pieces should not touch on the trays, or they will stick together.

Drying time: 6 to 12 hours

Temperature: 125°F

Consistency when dry: Flexible, not sticky

Blanching requirements: N/A

Oxidizing treatment: Use lemon juice dip if you wish to keep the bright color.

How to rehydrate: Spray until plump, or eat dry as snacks.

Consistency when rehydrated: Like fresh

Yield: 2 cups fresh kiwi = 1 cup dried kiwi = 1½ cups rehydrated kiwi

Lettuce

We often have excess lettuce during the growing season, and it seems a shame to relegate it all to the compost bin. Some of the specialty spring mixes can become quite bitter once dried, so experiment to find the type of lettuce that suits your needs. Also, skip drying iceberg lettuce. It has very little nutritional value and is not worth the dehydrator space used to dry it. Lettuce is not typically rehydrated.

Clean: For nonorganic lettuce, follow the cleaning tips on page 35. For organic lettuce, wash with cool water and pat dry.

How to prepare: Separate leaves from the head and remove thick stems or thick veins; they will slow the drying time.

Suggested thickness: Single leaves or half leaves

Drying time: Four to six hours

Temperature: 110°F

Consistency when dry: Papery

Blanching requirements: N/A

Oxidizing treatment: N/A

How to rehydrate: Use as powder for smoothies or in green powder blend.

Consistency when rehydrated: N/A

Yield: 1 cup fresh lettuce = ¼ cup dehydrated lettuce leaf = approximately 1 tablespoon powdered lettuce leaf

Mangoes or Papayas

These flavorful treats have become a staple for morning yogurt toppings. Rehydrated mango and papaya can be used in smoothies or made into syrup.

Clean: For nonorganic mangoes or papaya, follow the cleaning tips on page 35. Wash organic fruits with warm water, then dry.

How to prepare: Remove skin with a vegetable peeler, then cut flesh into large flat sections from top to bottom. A mandoline works well for this because the fruit is slippery.

Suggested thickness: ⅜-inch slices or wedges. Use parchment paper to reduce sticking. Pieces will stick to dehydrator trays if sliced too thin.

Drying time: 6 to 12 hours

Temperature: 125°F

Consistency when dry: Flexible and papery, not sticky

Blanching requirements: N/A

Oxidizing treatment: If preferred, spray with lemon juice as you are adding to trays.

How to rehydrate: Place in a bowl and cover with boiling water for 15 minutes.

Consistency when rehydrated: Like fresh

Yield: 2 cups fresh mango = 1 cup dried mango = 1½ cups rehydrated mango

Melons

We never can grow enough melons to keep the kids happy, so we purchase them during peak season and then dehydrate them. You'll find that a few long slices of dry honeydew or cantaloupe are perfect for an afternoon snack.

Clean: Wash the outside of organic and nonorganic melon with dish soap and warm water and pat dry.

How to prepare: For melon dices, remove flesh from the rind and cut into even pieces. For slices, cut the melon in half and remove seeds. Cut the melon into eight sections, remove the rind, and slice each eighth into five pieces.

Suggested thickness: ¼- to ½-inch-thick slices, 1½-inch dices

Drying time: 8 to 10 hours

Temperature: 125°F

Consistency when dry: Pliable, with dry centers

Blanching requirements: N/A

Oxidizing treatment: N/A

How to rehydrate: Not usually rehydrated; eaten dried as snacks or as a garnish in oatmeal or yogurt.

Consistency when rehydrated: Soft

Yield: 2 cups fresh melon = 1 cup dried melon = 1½ cups rehydrated melon

Mushrooms

Some cooks would never think of preserving food in their kitchen without first washing it. Mushrooms may be the exception. Wet mushrooms will turn black and not dry well. But mushrooms are grown commercially in a soilless medium of sterilized hardwood sawdust or straw, so they are sanitary to eat without washing. For those that have a texture aversion to mushrooms, you can dry and process them to a powder.

The flavor released by mushrooms is called umami and adds depth to soups, stews, meatloaf, burger patties, and omelets.

Clean: Wash with cool water and air dry for one hour before processing. Or, skip the washing and remove any growing medium with a towel or soft brush.

How to prepare: Remove woody stems and set aside to make mushroom powder.

Suggested thickness: Small mushrooms can be dried whole; large ones should be cut into ⅜-inch slices. Purchase them pre-sliced when they're on sale, and save yourself time.

Drying time: Four to eight hours

Temperature: 125°F

Consistency when dry: Brittle

Blanching requirements: N/A

Oxidizing treatment: N/A

How to rehydrate: Use as powder or add directly to your dish during cooking.

Consistency when rehydrated: Like cooked

Yield: 1 cup sliced, fresh mushrooms = ½ cup dehydrated mushrooms = 1 teaspoon of mushroom powder

Onions (Yellow, White, Red, Sweet)

Onions are a staple in many home-cooked meals. You can store them in a pantry for a few months by hanging fresh onions in a mesh bag or pantyhose. For long-term storage, dehydrating is the only option. Buy them in bulk during peak season, August through December, and be sure to give them their own dehydrator time, as their unique flavor can taint other foods.

Clean: Treat organic and nonorganic onions the same. Wash with cool water, and dry.

How to prepare: Remove papery outer layer and cut into rings.

Suggested thickness: ½-inch pieces, sliced, chopped, or minced, depending on how it will be used.

Drying time: 10 to 14 hours

Temperature: 125°F

Consistency when dry: Brittle

Blanching requirements: Blanch 15 to 30 seconds in boiling water to speed up drying time. Skip blanching if you are making onion powder.

Oxidizing treatment: None, although sweet onions may turn yellow or pink. The color goes away once rehydrated.

How to rehydrate: Add onion directly to pot when cooking meals, or grind to make powder.

Consistency when rehydrated: Like fresh

Yield: 2 cups fresh onion = 1 cup dried onion = 1¼ cups rehydrated onion

---

Diced onions will easily fall through dehydrator tray holes. Dry them in 2- to 3-inch-long slices or rings and easily mince them in a food processor once they are completely dry.

Peaches or Nectarines

Use dried fruit as a healthy snack alternative. I prefer drying nectarines, mostly because I do not enjoy the process of removing the skin from peaches. Peach cobbler is mighty tasty, though, and might get me to reconsider. They are also great when cooked, pureed, and added to fruit leather. For another twist, try the Honey Peach BBQ Sauce (page 127).

Clean: For nonorganic peaches or nectarines, follow the cleaning tips on page 35. Wash organic fruits with warm water, then dry.

How to prepare: Peel if desired. Remove pit.

Suggested thickness: Cut into quarters or eighths. Lay on dehydrator sheets, not touching.

Drying time: 10 to 15 hours

Temperature: 125°F

Consistency when dry: Leathery

Blanching requirements: If removing skin from peaches, blanch for one minute in boiling water until the skin blisters.

Oxidizing treatment: Use lemon juice or ascorbic acid.

How to rehydrate: Pour boiling water over the dried fruits until just covered and let soak for 30 minutes, or until they rehydrate to the consistency you are seeking.

Consistency when rehydrated: Firm, like fresh

Yield: 2 cups fresh peaches or nectarines = 1 cup dried peaches or nectarines = 1¼ cups rehydrated peaches or nectarines

Pears

Interchangeable with apples at our house, pears can be rehydrated and made into a tasty spiced butter (try Slow Cooker Spiced Pear Butter on page 128) or used fresh to make fruit leather.

Clean: For nonorganic pears, follow the cleaning tips on page 35. Wash organic peaches with cool water, then dry.

How to prepare: Remove stems, and peel if desired. Slice and remove tough center and seeds.

Suggested thickness: Halves, quarters, or eighths

Drying time: 12 to 24 hours, depending on slice thickness

Temperature: 125°F

Consistency when dry: Leathery

Blanching requirements: Blanch for two minutes in place of oxidizing treatment.

Oxidizing treatment: Use ascorbic dip to keep from browning, if not blanching.

How to rehydrate: Pour boiling water over the dried pears until just covered and let soak for 30 minutes. Add more water if necessary.

Consistency when rehydrated: Like fresh cooked

Yield: 2 cups fresh pears = 1 cup dried pears = 1½ cups rehydrated pears

Peas and Chickpeas

Peas are a fantastic addition to your food storage plan. Each cup has very little fat and 8 grams of protein. If you purchase frozen peas, you can add them directly to the dehydrator trays and skip all the processing time. Canned peas are also a quick option, if you don't mind the taste.

Clean: Shell organic and nonorganic fresh peas and wash with warm water; drain and rinse canned peas; add frozen peas directly to trays.

How to prepare: Remove fresh peas from the pod.

Suggested thickness: N/A

Drying time: 8 to 12 hours

Temperature: 125°F

Consistency when dry: Hard

Blanching requirements: Steam or boil fresh peas for four minutes.

Oxidizing treatment: N/A

How to rehydrate: Add directly to soup or stew, or cover and soak in cool water for one hour.

Consistency when rehydrated: Like fresh

Yield: 3 cups fresh peas = 1 cup dried peas = 3 cups rehydrated peas

Peanut (Raw)

Unshelled raw peanuts that have been properly cured can be stored in airtight containers and will keep for up to a year. Follow the instructions below to get them ready for drying. Once you have prepared the peanuts for dehydrating, you can make roasted peanuts and Homemade Roasted Peanut Butter (page 129).

How to clean and prepare: Shell and soak 4 cups of raw peanuts in warm water with 1 tablespoon of kosher or sea salt for 12 to 24 hours. Drain and rinse. Place on dehydrator sheets in a single layer. Turn nuts at least once during the processing.

Suggested thickness: N/A

Drying time: 12 to 24 hours

Temperature: 155°F

Consistency when dry: Brittle

Blanching requirements: N/A

Oxidizing treatment: N/A

How to rehydrate: N/A, roast for snacking and making nut butter.

Consistency when rehydrated: N/A

Yield: 4 cups raw peanuts = 4 cups dehydrated peanuts = 4 cups rehydrated peanuts

Peppers (Hot, Sweet)

We grow as many of these as we can each year. They dehydrate wonderfully and keep in the pantry for long-term storage. We add diced peppers to our morning eggs: To a 10-inch skillet, add a handful of peppers and cover with water. Simmer until the water evaporates and then cook your eggs as usual.

Clean: For nonorganic peppers, follow the cleaning tips on page 35. For organic peppers, wash with warm water and pat dry.

How to prepare: Wash, stem, and core. Remove the pith and seeds. Protect eyes and hands if cutting hot peppers.

Suggested thickness: ⅜-inch disks or ½-inch dices

Drying time: 8 to 12 hours

Temperature: 125°F

Consistency when dry: Leathery to brittle

Blanching requirements: N/A

Oxidizing treatment: N/A

How to rehydrate: Soak 1 cup dried pepper in 2 cups water for 1 hour then drain, or simmer peppers in water for 10 to 15 minutes.

Consistency when rehydrated: Like fresh cooked

Yield: 2 cups fresh peppers = 1 cup dried peppers = 1½ cups rehydrated peppers

Pineapple

We use a lot of pineapple in our morning smoothies, and fresh pineapple is a treat when it is in season and a good price. If you can't find fresh pineapple, look for frozen or canned fruit packed in its own juice when it goes on sale. You control the sugar content when you make it yourself. Add pineapple powder to smoothies, eat it dry as a snack, or rehydrate for a fresh-tasting treat. For a delicious dessert, try Steve's Low-Fat Pineapple Cake on page 172.

Clean: Fresh organic or nonorganic pineapple should be washed with warm water and dried.

How to prepare: Remove top and bottom, quarter the flesh, and remove core and tough skin.

Suggested thickness: ½-inch cubes, ¼-inch slices, or crushed. Strive for uniformity on the trays, keeping like sizes together.

Drying time: 8 to 16 hours, depending on size of cuts

Temperature: 125° to 135°F

Consistency when dry: Brittle

Blanching requirements: N/A

Oxidizing treatment: N/A

How to rehydrate: Soak in cool water until plump.

Consistency when rehydrated: Like fresh

Yield: 2 cups fresh pineapple = 1 cup dehydrated pineapple = 1½ cups rehydrated pineapple = ¼ cup pineapple powder

Plums

Years ago, we had a plum tree that was completely unappreciated by our family. It continued to put out fruit each year without fail, and we did not see its potential until years after we had it removed. Think of all the jam we missed, what a waste! Use very ripe plums for the sweetest finished product: prunes.

Clean: For nonorganic plums, follow the cleaning tips on page 35. Wash organic plums with warm water, then dry.

How to prepare: Half or quarter the plum and remove the pit. Lay plums on trays skin side down, not touching.

Suggested thickness: Use quarters, which will dry faster than halves.

Drying time: 24+ hours

Temperature: 125° F

Consistency when dry: Leathery, pliable

Blanching requirements: Place in boiling water for 30 seconds to soften the skin.

Oxidizing treatment: Use lemon juice or ascorbic acid, if you'd like, for lighter colored fruit.

How to rehydrate: Place dried plums and water in a saucepan; bring to a boil. Cover, reduce heat, and simmer for 10 minutes, or until very tender.

Consistency when rehydrated: Like cooked

Yield: 2 cups fresh plums = 1 cup dried plums = 1½ cups rehydrated plums

Make prune powder. Cut the pieces into smaller sizes if you plan to powder the plums, and use the powder in smoothies.

Potatoes

Another staple of the prepared pantry, potatoes are so versatile that you don't want to be without them. The lowly potato keeps for four to six months in a properly ventilated root cellar; however, most of us don't have the luxury of an on-site cellar. For long-term storage of up to five years, dehydrate the potatoes. I find that it's best to have a use in mind before I dehydrate: Does the finished recipe need slices, shreds, or cubes? Shredded potatoes can be used in most recipes; try Hash Brown Mix in a Jar on page 162.

Any type of potato can be dehydrated. However, you may find that those with waxy skin, like yellow, white, and red potatoes will dry and rehydrate the best. If you are using frozen potatoes, it is not necessary to do the blanching process before dehydrating.

You might find that the center of the potato turns black after dehydrating. This happens when the outside dries quicker than the center. These potatoes are still OK to eat, but should not be stored long term.

Clean: For organic and nonorganic potatoes, scrub clean with hot water and a vegetable brush.

How to prepare: Keep peel for added nutrients. After cooking, process into slices, cubes, or shreds.

Suggested thickness: ⅛-inch round slices, ⅓-inch cubes, shreds

Drying time: 8 to 16 hours

Temperature: 125° to 135°F

Consistency when dry: Brittle, transparent

Blanching requirements: Boil for five to six minutes so a knife can be inserted partway through the potato.

Oxidizing treatment: Dip white potatoes in lemon juice or ascorbic acid.

How to rehydrate: Add directly to soup or stew, along with additional water; alternatively, soak in hot water for 30 minutes.

Consistency when rehydrated: Like fresh

Yield: 2 cups fresh diced potatoes = 1 cup dried potatoes = 1¼ cups rehydrated potatoes

Raspberries and Blackberries

I grew up in the Pacific Northwest, where the berries of summer have names like loganberry, blackberry, salmonberry, boysenberry, and marionberry. If you happen to live in berry country, you know these are the tastiest when purchased right from the farmer. Now that I live in Texas, these berries are expensive, and the quality does not compare. I rarely purchase them at the store and instead choose to purchase frozen berries. Next time I go back to Oregon in July, I'm going to dehydrate batches and batches of berries and FedEx them home!

Clean: For nonorganic berries, follow the cleaning tips on page 35. If possible, do not wash, because these berries are fragile. Completely air dry before dehydrating, because wet berries will not retain their shape during the drying process.

How to prepare: Stand berries on their flat end to dry all sides. Use dehydrator sheets; they will drip as they dry and you'll have juice on the trays below.

Suggested thickness: Dry whole

Drying time: 15 to 20 hours, depending on size

Temperature: 125° F

Consistency when dry: Brittle, or crushed to a powder

Blanching requirements: N/A

Oxidizing treatment: N/A

How to rehydrate: Mist with a spray bottle to retain shape; simmer in juice or water for pie filling. Make berry powder for smoothies.

Consistency when rehydrated: Like fresh cooked

Yield: 2 cups fresh berries = 1 cup dried berries = 1¼ cups rehydrated berries

Rhubarb

An old favorite once found in every kitchen garden, rhubarb is enjoying a boost in popularity as a home garden crop. It thrives in cold climates, where the ground freezes in the winter. The roots and leaves are poisonous and should not be eaten. The tender stalks are used for jam, pies, and as a condiment sauce, often combined with berries.

Clean: For nonorganic rhubarb, follow the cleaning tips on page 35. For organic rhubarb, wash with warm water and pat dry well.

How to prepare: Discard leaves, then cut stem into equal-size pieces.

Suggested thickness: ½-inch to 1-inch pieces

Drying time: 8 to 12 hours

Temperature: 135° F

Consistency when dry: Brittle

Blanching requirements: Steam five minutes or boil one minute until slightly tender. Dip in ice water to cool.

Oxidizing treatment: N/A

How to rehydrate: Soak in hot water until plump.

Consistency when rehydrated: Like fresh

Yield: 2½ cups fresh rhubarb = 1 cup dried rhubarb = 1½ cups rehydrated rhubarb

Spinach

Just like preserving lettuce, drying spinach leaves may seem like a strange thing to do. After all, the yield for 1 cup of spinach leaves is only 1 tablespoon of spinach powder. However, the health benefits of adding powdered spinach to smoothies, soups, and baked goods make it well worth your time. We purchase large bags of organic spinach at the local big box store, eat as much as we can, and then dehydrate the rest. This method makes spinach cost-effective, and nothing goes to waste.

Clean: For nonorganic spinach, follow the cleaning tips on page 35. For organic spinach, wash with cool water and pat dry.

How to prepare: If using for cooking, remove stems. If powdering, leave whole.

Suggested thickness: Whole leaves

Drying time: Four to six hours

Temperature: 110°F

Consistency when dry: Brittle

Blanching requirements: N/A

Oxidizing treatment: N/A

How to rehydrate: Add 1 cup dried spinach to 1 cup water and soak for half an hour. Alternatively, add directly to a recipe, or powder for baking.

Consistency when rehydrated: Like cooked

Yield: 2 cups fresh spinach = 1 cup dried spinach = 1½ cups rehydrated spinach = 1 tablespoon spinach powder

Strawberries

Strawberries are at the top of the EWG's "Dirty Dozen" list of fruit with the most pesticides. Unless you are purchasing organic or growing your own crop, it will be especially important to clean them thoroughly before drying them. If you don't have a source for fresh berries, frozen strawberries dry exceptionally well, but they will not hold their shape like fresh berries do after drying.

Clean: For nonorganic strawberries, follow the cleaning tips on page 35. For organic berries, wash with warm water and pat dry lightly.

How to prepare: Remove tops and soft spots.

Suggested thickness: Cut small to medium berries in half. Cut large berries into quarters.

Drying time: 8 to 16 hours

Temperature: 125°F

Consistency when dry: Pliable, dry in center

Blanching requirements: N/A

Oxidizing treatment: Use lemon juice or ascorbic acid, if you'd like, for lighter colored fruit.

How to rehydrate: Soak in hot water or warmed juice for 15 to 20 minutes, or simmer in water on the stovetop until the fruit is plump and has absorbed the water.

Consistency when rehydrated: Plump, but mushy. Best for sauces or shortcake.

Yield: 2½ cups fresh strawberries = 1 cup dried strawberries = 1 cup rehydrated strawberries

Summer Squash

An end-of-season garden often has an abundance of summer squash. We grow traditional zucchini, yellow crookneck, and pattypan each year, and then we cut them into cubes or shredded pieces for soup. They also make healthy chips. The Zucchini Chips recipe on page 146 is so popular that it's hard to keep them around the house. We change up the spices to fit the mood, and they are made with no oil, so the calories are minimal.

Clean: For both organic and nonorganic squash, wash using natural soap and warm water, then towel dry.

How to prepare: Cut off the ends, then use a mandoline to cut uniform slices.

Suggested thickness: ⅛- to ¼-inch rounds for chips, or ½-inch cubes

Drying time: 10 to 12 hours for chips, 12 to 18 hours for cubes

Temperature: 125°F

Consistency when dry: Crisp

Blanching requirements: N/A

Oxidizing treatment: N/A

How to rehydrate: Soak in warm water 15 minutes, drop whole into soup, or eat as chips.

Consistency when rehydrated: Like cooked

Yield: 2 cups fresh summer squash = 1 cup dried summer squash = 1½ cups rehydrated summer squash

Sweet Potatoes and Yams

Sweet potatoes are high in beta carotene, magnesium, calcium, potassium, and iron, as well as vitamins E and C. Just the things you'd like to have in a shelf-stable food storage plan! They will last three to five weeks in a dark, cool pantry and two to three months in the refrigerator. Dehydrating brings their storage time to as much as five years. For more ways to enjoy these tubers, try Sweet Potato Chips (page 144), Sweet Potato Powder (page 132), and mashed sweet potatoes (page 133), all of which can be made with yams too.

Clean: Scrub organic and nonorganic sweet potatoes clean with a vegetable brush and warm water, then pat dry.

How to prepare: Leave the skins on for added fiber, or peel and grate, slice, or cube.

Suggested thickness: ⅛-inch round slices; ⅓-inch cubes; shreds. Cut when cold.

Drying time: 8 to 16 hours

Temperature: 125°F

Consistency when dry: Brittle

Blanching requirements: Steam or boil until completely cooked. Cool in refrigerator overnight.

Oxidizing treatment: N/A

How to rehydrate: Add 1 cup dried sweet potatoes to 2 cups boiling water, soak for an hour. Alternatively, add cubes directly to a soup, or eat chips dried.

Consistency when rehydrated: Like freshly cooked

Yield: 2 cups fresh sweet potatoes = 1 cup dried sweet potatoes = 1½ cups rehydrated sweet potatoes

Tomatoes

Everyone wants to have tomatoes in their prepper food storage. It is the most versatile fruit you can store. We dry tomato pieces with the skin on and use them to make powder. The powder is then rehydrated to make paste and sauce. I find it quicker to dry them than to go through the whole process of blanching and skin peeling (something I heartily dislike), which is needed when you process them in a water bath canner.

Clean: For nonorganic tomatoes, follow the cleaning tips on page 35. For organic tomatoes, wash with warm water and pat dry.

How to prepare: Optionally, remove the skins by blanching. Core tomatoes and remove tomato ends.

Suggested thickness: Cut stewing or slicing tomatoes into quarters; cut cherry tomatoes in half.

Drying time: 8 to 12 hours

Temperature: 135°F

Consistency when dry: Leathery to brittle

Blanching requirements: With a knife, cut an X on the bottom of the tomato, just deep enough to penetrate the skin. Drop tomato into boiling water. Blanch for 20 to 30 seconds. Use a slotted spoon to remove tomato from boiling water. Immerse tomato in ice water. Use a knife to remove the tomato core. Skin will slip off.

Oxidizing treatment: N/A

How to rehydrate: Place tomatoes in a bowl and cover with cool water for 30 to 60 minutes, then drain. Alternatively, add a small amount of cool water to individual tomato pieces with a spray bottle. Continue this every 15 minutes or so until the fruit has plumped up.

Consistency when rehydrated: Soft, like cooked

Yield: 2 cups fresh tomatoes = 1 cup dried tomatoes = 1½ cups rehydrated tomatoes = ⅔ cup tomato powder

---

You can use shelf-stable tomato powder to make these common tomato products:

- *Tomato paste = Equal amounts tomato powder + water*

- *Tomato sauce = 1 part tomato powder + 3 parts water*

- *Tomato soup = 1 part tomato powder + 1 part water + 2 parts cream*

- *Tomato juice = 1 teaspoon tomato powder + ½ cup water*

Watermelon

Dehydrating a watermelon is not something that readily comes to mind, but if you are looking for a tasty snack that brings a bit of summer into your winter diet, this is it. You can store this long-term for more than a year (if you can keep it around that long) by first putting your dehydrated fruit in the freezer for two weeks to pasteurize it, and then by vacuum packing it in serving-size packages, with oxygen absorbers in each bag. Place the vacuum-packed bags in a storage container out of direct light.

Clean: Wash the rind of organic or nonorganic watermelon with soap and warm water, and dry.

How to prepare: Slice the melon into ½-inch-thick rounds. Cut meat away from the rinds and cut into 2- to 3-inch pieces. Discard seeds.

Suggested thickness: ½-inch rounds

Drying time: 8 to 12 hours

Temperature: 125°F

Consistency when dry: Like fruit leather

Blanching requirements: N/A

Oxidizing treatment: N/A

How to rehydrate: Not typically rehydrated; eaten as a dry snack.

Consistency when rehydrated: N/A

Yield: 2 cups fresh watermelon = ½ cup dehydrated watermelon = 1½ cups rehydrated watermelon

---

Black watermelon seeds can be made into a tasty snack similar to sunflower seeds. Rinse seeds to remove watermelon pulp and place on a dehydrator tray for two hours at 140°F, until completely dry. Place the dry seeds in a frying pan over medium heat and continually turn until roasted. Add 1 cup water and 1 tablespoon salt, then stir until evaporated. Allow them to cool completely before shelling and eating.

Winter Squash (Pumpkin, Acorn, Butternut, Delicata)

Winter squash is shelf stable for many months in the root cellar or in a cold, dark area of your pantry, but it will rapidly deteriorate if stored below 50°F. If you grow more than you can store, dehydrating is a viable option. The advantages of using a dehydrator to preserve your winter squash are threefold: The finished product is lightweight, it requires little storage space, and it will keep for many years if stored away from direct light and heat.

Winter squash varieties include acorn, buttercup, butternut, banana, golden delicious, Hubbard, and sweet meat. Dehydrated pumpkin and other winter squash cubes work well for soups and sautés (Sautéed Winter Squash with Apples on page 156). Dried and rehydrated cubes do not work well for pies and other recipes, like leathers (try Pumpkin Pie Leather on page 140); it is hard to get the correct consistency because of case hardening, so purees work better. Shredded squash dries well in small bird-nest serving sizes; try making Garlic Creole Spiced Squash Nests (page 158).

Clean: Wash the outside of organic or nonorganic winter squash with soap and warm water, then towel dry.

How to prepare: Peel and seed the squash, then puree or cut into pieces. To puree, cut the squash in half and cook, cut side down, at 400°F until completely soft, 30 to 45 minutes. Scoop the pulp into a bowl and use an immersion blender to puree. Flatten the pulp onto Paraflexx sheets no more than ¼ inch thick.

Suggested thickness: Cut into ¼-inch cubes or ¼-inch-thick strips, 1 to 2 inches long. Alternatively, puree or shred.

Drying time: 8 to 12 hours

Temperature: 140°F for two to three hours, then reduce temperature to 130°F and continue drying until squash is tough and brittle, three to six hours.

Consistency when dry: Brittle

Blanching requirements: Boil for three minutes.

Oxidizing treatment: N/A

How to rehydrate: Pour boiling water over the dehydrated squash pieces and let soak for 30 minutes before draining and proceeding with your recipe. Save the soaking liquid to use in soups. Drop bird-nest shreds into boiling water. Or, for fruit leather, pour boiling water over pieces cut into 1-inch squares, then mix until it reaches the consistency you are looking for.

Consistency when rehydrated: Like freshly blanched

Yield: 2½ cups fresh winter squash = 1 cup dried winter squash = 2 cups rehydrated winter squash

CHAPTER 10

RECIPES

BLUEBERRY BASIL SYRUP

Making a syrup from dehydrated fruit is a great way to extend the usefulness of your pantry. Plus, who doesn't like warm blueberries on their Sunday morning pancakes? You can swap blueberries for any fruit, omit or replace the herbs in this recipe, or substitute store-bought juice instead of processing fresh fruit into juice. It's that versatile!

Yield: 3 cups   **Prep time:** 10 minutes   **Cook time:** 10 minutes

2 cups dehydrated blueberries

2 cups sugar

¼ cup dried basil leaves

⅛ teaspoon ascorbic acid

1. To make blueberry juice, cook the dehydrated blueberries in 2½ cups water in a nonreactive pan. Bring to a boil and simmer for 10 minutes, stirring and mashing the fruit as it cooks. Strain through a colander to remove the berries. Set aside berries.

2. Combine the blueberry juice, sugar, and basil leaves in a saucepan, and bring to a full boil. Reduce the heat and simmer for 5 minutes. Skim off any foam.

3. Remove saucepan from the heat and strain out the basil leaves.

4. Optionally, if you like blueberry pieces in your syrup, return the strained syrup to the saucepan and add back the berries. Simmer for 2 minutes.

5. Remove saucepan from heat and add ascorbic acid. Stir to combine.

6. Pour the finished syrup into sterilized jars, seal, and label. This syrup can be used immediately or stored in swing-top bottles for up to a year with ascorbic acid added, or 6 months without it. Reducing the sugar content will reduce the shelf life. You can store any opened bottles in the refrigerator for up to 2 weeks.

PECTIN WITH CITRUS PITH

Dehydrating citrus can leave you with a lot of pith (that white, bitter substance under the flavorful rind), which is high in pectin. Most food preservation techniques call for composting the pith, but you can turn it into homemade pectin for thickening jam and jelly. Any citrus works for this recipe, and you can freeze small amounts of pith until you have enough for a batch. Looking for citrus with a lot of pith? It's all about the skin thickness. Thick-skinned citrus fruits will have a lot of pith inside.

Yield: 2 cups **Prep time:** 5 minutes **Cook time:** 20 minutes, plus rest time

½ pound citrus pith and seeds
¼ cup citrus juice, such as lemon

1. Use a vegetable peeler to remove the skin from the fruit. Save the skin for dehydrating.

2. Use a vegetable peeler to remove the pith. Chop the pith and set it aside, along with the seeds.

3. Add pith, seeds, and citrus juice to a medium, nonreactive pot. Let pot stand for an hour.

4. Add 2 cups water and let it stand another hour.

5. Bring the ingredients of the pot to a boil over high heat. Reduce heat, and simmer for 15 minutes. Cool to room temperature.

6. Place mixture in a jelly bag and allow it to drain. Press to remove juice.

7. Store extra pectin in the freezer.

The Pectin Test

Pour 1 teaspoon of homemade pectin into a glass cup. Add 1 teaspoon of rubbing alcohol and shake gently. If the pectin forms a solid jelly clot, it is ready to use in a recipe on a one-to-one ratio with sugar.

PINK GRAPEFRUIT JELLY

Yield: 2 cups   **Prep time:** 15 minutes   **Cook time:** 30 minutes

4 handfuls dehydrated pink grapefruit peels or rounds

2 cups cool water

1½ cups sugar

1. Place grapefruit peels or rounds in a large bowl and cover with cool water until plump, about 15 minutes. Drain and reserve the grapefruit liquid.

2. Chop the rehydrated grapefruit into small pieces.

3. Measure ½ pound of the chopped grapefruit pieces, and add to a nonreactive pot along with the reserved water and sugar. Add enough water to cover the grapefruit pieces, if needed. Boil until thoroughly cooked, 30 minutes.

4. Drain through a jelly bag. Allow to slightly cool and press out all liquid.

GINGER AND LEMON INFUSED HONEY

It's best to use dried herbs for this recipe. To reduce the risk of adding bacteria to the infused honey, you must wash and completely dry off any fresh herbs or spices you plan on using. Use this recipe when you feel a cold coming on, as it is very soothing.

Yield: 1 cup   **Prep time:** 5 minutes, plus 2-week wait time

1 tablespoon dried ginger

1 teaspoon dried citrus peel

1 cup raw, unfiltered, unpasteurized honey, slightly warmed

1. Place the dried ginger and citrus into a coffee grinder and chop to release the aromatic flavors.

2. Place the ginger and citrus in a tea bag or square of cheesecloth and tie with string so the bag/cheesecloth will remain closed. (It is almost impossible to pick dried herbs out of honey.)

3. In a pint jar, pour three quarters of the slightly warmed honey over the top of the herb bag. Use a chopstick or skewer to stir the honey, remove air bubbles, and make sure the herb bag is completely moistened.

4. Top off the jar with the remaining honey. Screw the lid on tightly. Place the jar out of direct sunlight, in an area where you will be able to monitor the process.

5. Allow the flavors to infuse for 2 weeks. If you have a problem with the spice bag floating to the surface, turn the jar upside down. This will keep the flavors submerged and to mix the honey ever so slightly.

6. After 2 weeks, remove the tea bag and store the honey in the pantry for up to a year.

HONEY PEACH BBQ SAUCE

Brush this sweet, spicy sauce over chicken or pork in the last few minutes of grilling. It thickens as it cools. Use less chipotle for a milder sauce.

Yield: 1 cup   **Prep time:** 30 minutes   **Cook time:** 20 minutes

16 slices dehydrated peaches or 1 cup fresh sliced peaches

2 teaspoons olive oil

1 cup chopped onion

1 teaspoon salt

1 teaspoon chipotle powder

¼ teaspoon ground cumin

pinch of allspice

¼ cup honey

4 teaspoons apple cider vinegar

1. Place peaches in a large bowl, cover with warm water, and soak for 30 minutes. Drain and discard soaking liquid. Roughly chop the rehydrated peaches. and set aside.

2. Coat the bottom of a medium saucepan with olive oil. Over medium heat, add onions and cook until softened and starting to brown, 5 minutes.

3. Add salt, chipotle, cumin, and allspice and cook until the spices smell fragrant, about 30 seconds.

4. Add rehydrated peaches, honey, and vinegar, and stir to coat.

5. Cover saucepan, increase heat to medium-high, and cook until the peaches are completely soft and breaking down, 15 minutes.

6. Transfer to a blender to puree, or use an immersion blender. Add additional apple cider vinegar for thinner sauce.

SLOW COOKER SPICED PEAR BUTTER

As an alternative, you can make the recipe with fresh pears and dehydrate the finished recipe. To reconstitute, add small amounts of boiling water until the butter reaches the consistency you want.

Yield: 3 cups   **Prep time:** 1 hour   **Cook time:** 4 to 8 hours

1 pound dehydrated pear sections (approximately 10 fresh pears)

¼ cup brown sugar

1 tablespoon cinnamon

1 teaspoon ground ginger

½ teaspoon ground nutmeg

1. Add the dehydrated pears to a slow cooker and add enough water to cover the fruit. With the lid off, cook on low for 1 hour until the pears rehydrate.

2. Add the remaining ingredients to the slow cooker, stir to combine, and cover.

3. Cook for 4 hours on high or 6 to 8 hours on low.

4. Use an immersion blender to puree the mixture, or transfer to a blender and blend in small batches.

5. Store in the refrigerator for up to 3 weeks.

HOMEMADE ROASTED PEANUT BUTTER

Enjoy this peanut butter as is, or experiment by adding dark chocolate powder, banana chips, white chocolate chips, maple, or coconut during the blending process. Did you know that raw peanuts taste like beans? For the best flavor, raw peanuts must be soaked and dehydrated before they are roasted for peanut butter.

Yield: ½ cup   **Prep time:** 20 minutes   **Cook time:** 5 minutes

2 cups dehydrated peanuts

honey, to taste

1. Preheat oven to 300° F.

2. Spread peanuts no more than ½ inch thick on a baking sheet. Roast for 20 minutes. When properly roasted, they will be slightly browned and have the taste of peanuts, nutty and pleasant, not like a bean.

3. In a food processor, grind the roasted peanuts until butter forms, approximately 5 minutes. Scrape the sides and add honey to taste, processing another minute until it reaches the consistency you want. Additional vegetable or peanut oil can be added if you want thinner peanut butter.

CREAMY CUCUMBER SALAD DRESSING

Yield: 2 cups **Prep time:** 15 minutes

1 cup dehydrated cucumber chips

½ cup dehydrated green onions

½ teaspoon dried garlic

¾ cup light sour cream

1 tablespoon light mayonnaise

1 tablespoon lemon juice

1 teaspoon dried dill weed, basil, or parsley

1. Place cucumber chips and onions in a large bowl, cover with cool water, and soak for 15 minutes. Drain and discard soaking liquid.

2. Blend the rehydrated vegetables and remaining ingredients in a blender or small food processor until smooth.

3. Add a splash of milk if the dressing needs to be thinned.

TOMATO POWDER

The drier your tomatoes, the easier they will be to powder. So if you intend to turn your dried tomatoes into a powder, you may want to dehydrate them for an extra hour or two than is recommended in the Tomatoes section on page 118. The entire process can take quite a bit of time and is entirely dependent on the quality of the grinder you use; I've found that a coffee grinder works best. It's worth it, however, to have a few cups of tomato powder on hand for quick cooking needs.

Yield: ⅔ cup   **Prep time:** 5 minutes

1 cup dehydrated tomatoes, divided

1. In ¼-cup batches, grind dehydrated tomatoes in a food processor, blender, or coffee grinder until tomatoes reach powder form.

2. Transfer to a mesh strainer and, using a spatula, move the pieces around until the powder falls through the mesh.

SWEET POTATO POWDER

Sweet potato powder rehydrates quickly using boiling water to create "instant" mashed sweet potatoes. It's great if you are making baby food, or want to serve a healthy side dish. Store the sweet potato powder in a jar and refrigerate for up to 1 month. For additional storage time, include a 100cc oxygen absorber in the jar, or vacuum-seal the jar with a FoodSaver jar attachment. Refrigerate for up to 3 months.

Yield: 2 cups mash, ½ cup powder   **Prep time:** 60 minutes
Cook time: 5 to 8 hours

2 pounds sweet potatoes

1. Peel sweet potatoes, or leave skins on for an added nutritional benefit. Cut into thin strips. Boil for 10 to 15 minutes, until the sweet potatoes are soft, then drain and reserve cooking liquid. Alternatively, bake whole and cut strips when cooked.

2. Mash the sweet potatoes to a smooth consistency. Thin with water, preferably cooking liquid, if necessary.

3. Spread ½ cup of potato mash on each Paraflexx sheet, plastic wrap–lined tray, or on fruit leather sheets. Spread VERY thin.

4. Dry at 135°F for 4 to 6 hours. When the top is dry, turn the sheets of sweet potatoes over, remove the tray wrap, and dry the underside for another 1 to 2 hours if necessary.

5. Stop drying when the sweet potato sheets are crispy, and the product crumbles.

6. Process into a powder by adding the dehydrated sweet potato bark into a blender or food processor and blending.

Other Uses for Sweet Potato Powder

• *Make instant mashed sweet potatoes by slowly adding hot water to powdered sweet potatoes until you reach a thick mashed-potato consistency. Add sugar and spices as needed.*

• *Make sweet potato biscuits by replacing ½ cup white flour with sweet potato flour.*

• *Add sweet potato powder to morning smoothies.*

• *Make morning porridge by combining 1 tablespoon sweet potato powder, dried fruit, and ½ cup quick oats with 1 cup boiling water.*

CELERY SALT

Use this salt for everyday cooking, canning, and even fermenting projects. Be sure to adjust your recipe for the salt content. Store celery salt in a canning jar, it will last for at least 1 year under normal pantry conditions.

Yield: 1 cup   **Prep time:** 5 minutes

½ cup dried celery stalks and leaves

½ cup kosher salt, plus more as needed

1. Grind the celery in a coffee grinder or food processor until finely ground.

2. Add the kosher salt and process in short bursts for a minute, until the mixture reaches the consistency you are looking for. Play around with the ratio of salt and celery to fit your taste.

GREEN POWDER BLEND

If you find yourself with extra greens in the crisper drawer, don't let them go to waste. Any greens will do. It's easy to make a green powder blend that uses these leftovers, and it will be every bit as healthy as eating fresh greens. You can use the powder in smoothies to add more greens to your diet. Store vegetables as individual powders or create a blend of your favorites.

Yield: 2 cups powder   **Prep time:** 5 minutes   **Cook time:** 4 to 8 hours

6 cups fresh spinach leaves
6 cups fresh kale leaves

1. It is not necessary to trim the vegetable leaves before dehydrating; however, you may want to remove tough ribs, stems, and seeds.

2. Dry vegetables at 100°F and begin checking for dryness at 4 hours. Depending on the size of the leaves and their thickness, this may take up to 8 hours.

3. Once dry, rub the leaves between your hands to break them into smaller pieces. Grind the pieces in a food processor, blender, or coffee grinder until greens reach powder form. Strain powder through a sieve. Re-blend any large pieces until it is all powdered.

Leftover Vegetables You Can Powder

- *beet and turnip tops*
- *bell peppers*
- *herb cuttings*
- *kale*
- *leeks and green onions*
- *lettuce greens*
- *spinach*
- *bok choi*

SHREDDED COCONUT

You really have to love fresh coconut to go through all the trouble of cracking, peeling, and shredding them! Use a small-holed or medium-holed grater for fine or regular shreds, a slicer for coconut chips, or a vegetable peeler for thicker chips.

Yield: 2 to 3 cups   **Prep time:** 20 minutes   **Cook time:** 6 to 10 hours

1 small fresh coconut, husked

1. Poke a hole in the top of the coconut and drain the milk.

2. Using a hammer, break the coconut in half along the center mark. Remove the hard outer shell.

3. Remove the soft outer membrane with a vegetable peeler or sharp knife.

4. Grate the fresh coconut meat in several ways.

5. Dry small and medium shreds on a dehydrator tray at 110°F for 6 to 8 hours. Thick coconut shreds may take up to 10 hours to finish.

COCONUT FLOUR

Sometimes it will be necessary to increase the amount of liquid used in a recipe that has coconut flour. Since coconut flour loves moisture, it will absorb additional liquid in a recipe. Store flour for up to 6 months in an airtight container, in a dark, cool cabinet until ready to use.

Yield: ½ cup   **Prep time:** 5 minutes   **Cook time:** 2 to 4 hours

1 cup Shredded Coconut (page 136)

2 cups water

1. Place the shredded coconut in a blender with 2 cups water. Process on high until the coconut is finely chopped.

2. Strain the milk through a jelly bag; save to drink.

3. Take the pulp, spread it on a dehydrator Paraflexx sheet, and dry it at 110°F for 2 to 4 hours.

4. Once dried, process the dehydrated pulp into a fine powder. This coconut flour will have less fat and also require more water or egg when used in recipes.

Variation: You can omit the water and process the shredded coconut in small batches in a blender until it is the consistency of a fine powder. This flour has a higher fat content and won't be as drying in recipes.

STRAWBERRY BANANA ROLLS

Most often used as snacks, fruit leather can also be rehydrated and used in pie fillings and dessert toppings, or made into a soup base with vegetables, bouillon, and spices. Use these for backpacking or emergency kit snacks.

Yield: 3 large trays, 24 rolls   **Prep time:** 10 minutes
Cook time: 6 to 8 hours

2 pounds strawberries, hulled

3 medium-size ripe bananas

honey (optional)

water or fruit juice, as needed

1. Cut the strawberries into quarters, then add to a blender.

2. Break bananas up into 2-inch pieces, then add to the blender.

3. Add honey to taste, if desired.

4. Following the no-cook directions for fruit leather on page 53, blend the fruit until smooth. Add water or juice in 1-tablespoon increments, as needed, to thin the mixture.

5. Cover dehydrator trays with a plastic fruit leather tray or plastic wrap. Spoon the mixture in equal amounts onto dehydrator trays. Cover with tray covers or plastic wrap. Dry at 125°F for 6 to 8 hours.

CINNAMON APPLE LEATHER

Yield: 4 large trays, 36 rolls   **Prep time:** 40 minutes
Cook time: 6 to 10 hours

8 sweet apples, peeled and cored

1 cup water

ground cinnamon, to taste

2 tablespoons lemon juice

sugar, to taste (optional)

1. Roughly chop the apples. Add apples and water to a large pot. Cover and simmer over medium-low heat for 15 minutes.

2. Mash the apples in the pot, then add cinnamon, lemon juice, and sugar, if using. Simmer for 10 minutes.

3. Allow mixture to cool, then run small batches of apples through a blender or food mill until a consistent puree forms.

4. Cover dehydrator trays with a plastic fruit leather tray or plastic wrap. Spread the puree onto dehydrator trays to form a ¼-inch-thick layer. Cover with tray covers or plastic wrap. Dry at 125° F for 6 to 10 hours.

PUMPKIN PIE LEATHER

Yield: 3 large trays, 24 rolls
Prep time: 5 to 20 minutes if using canned pumpkin; 40 to 60 minutes for fresh pumpkin
Cook time: 8 to 10 hours

1 (29-ounce) can pumpkin or 3 cups fresh pumpkin, cooked and pureed

¼ cup honey

¼ cup applesauce

2 teaspoons ground cinnamon

½ teaspoon ground nutmeg

½ teaspoon powdered cloves

½ teaspoon ground ginger

1. Mix all the ingredients in a large bowl until puree forms.

2. Cover dehydrator trays with a plastic fruit leather tray or plastic wrap. Spread the puree onto dehydrator trays to form a ¼-inch-thick layer. Cover with tray covers or plastic wrap. Dry at 130°F for 8 to 10 hours.

PIZZA BLEND TOMATO LEATHER

If you have extra tomatoes at harvest time, think about making pizza-seasoned leather. This tomato leather can be made plain and rehydrated to make sauce, or you can use the Pizza Seasoning Blend, below, to add flavor.

Yield: 2 large trays, 16 rolls **Prep time:** 40 minutes
Cook time: 8 to 12 hours

1 pound tomatoes, cored and quartered

½ tablespoon Pizza Seasoning Blend (optional)

1. Cook the tomatoes in a covered medium saucepan over low heat for 15 to 20 minutes. Remove from heat and let cool for a few minutes.

2. Puree the cooked tomatoes in a blender or food processor until smooth. Add seasoning, if using, and blend.

3. Return the puree to the saucepan and heat until the water has evaporated and the sauce has thickened.

4. Cover dehydrator trays with a plastic fruit leather tray or plastic wrap. Spread the tomato puree onto dehydrator trays to form a ¼-inch-thick layer. Cover with tray covers or plastic wrap. Dry at 135°F for 8 to 12 hours.

PIZZA SEASONING BLEND

1½ teaspoons dried basil

1½ teaspoons dried oregano

1½ teaspoons dried onion

1½ teaspoons dried rosemary

½ teaspoon dried thyme

½ teaspoon garlic powder

½ teaspoon salt

½ teaspoon red pepper flakes

Mix together and run through a spice mill or coffee grinder to get a powder. Use ½ tablespoon per pound of tomatoes.

MIXED VEGETABLE LEATHER

Yield: 1 large tray, 8 rolls   **Prep time:** 40 minutes   **Cook time:** 4 to 8 hours

2 cups tomatoes, cored and cut into chunks

1 small onion, chopped

¼ cup chopped celery

1 sprig basil

salt, to taste

1. Cook all the ingredients in a covered medium saucepan over low heat for 15 to 20 minutes. Remove from heat and let cool for a few minutes.

2. Add to a blender and puree until smooth.

3. Return the puree to the saucepan and heat until the water has evaporated and the sauce has thickened.

4. Cover dehydrator trays with a plastic fruit leather tray or plastic wrap. Spread the puree onto dehydrator trays to form a ¼-inch-thick layer. Cover with tray covers or plastic wrap. Dry at 135°F, until it is pliable (for a wrap), about 4 hours, or until crisp (to use in soups and casseroles), 6 to 8 hours.

TOMATO WRAPS

This vegetable leather does not require cooking. Use as a wrap for snacks, or around meat and cheese. Try this method with other vegetables, like cucumber, spinach, zucchini, yellow squash, eggplant, or carrot. Experiment with adding spices, peppers, onions, garlic, ground flax, or chia seed.

Yield: 2 large trays, 6 wraps   **Prep time:** 5 minutes   **Cook time:** 4 hours

2 pounds tomatoes, cored and chopped

seasonings, to taste

1. Puree the fresh tomatoes in a blender or food processor until smooth.

2. Add seasoning as desired.

3. Cover dehydrator trays with a plastic fruit leather tray or plastic wrap. Spread the puree onto dehydrator trays to form a ¼-inch-thick layer. Cover with tray covers or plastic wrap. Dry at 125°F until pliable and able to remove from the trays, but not crisp, about 4 hours.

SWEET POTATO CHIPS

My family enjoys sweet potato chips, a healthy alternative to store-bought potato chips. Some people recommend making these chips without cooking the potatoes, but I don't. Without precooking, the chips will be hard as a rock, and impossible to eat. Season chips with your favorite flavors. Try sugar, cinnamon, and nutmeg; salt, pepper, and onion powder; or salt and smoked paprika. Alternatively, you can leave the chips "naked" and rehydrate them to use in soups and stews.

Yield: 6 cups **Prep time:** 15 minutes **Cook time:** 4 to 8 hours

4 large sweet potatoes

1. Peel potatoes, or leave skins on for an added nutritional benefit.

2. Using a mandoline, slice each potato into ⅛-inch-thick rounds.

3. Add the rounds to a large pot of boiling water and cook until just soft, about 10 minutes. Drain and discard liquid. Do not overcook; they should retain their shape when handled.

4. Lay wet sweet potato rounds on dehydrator trays. They should not touch.

5. Sprinkle salt and seasoning on chip rounds (optional).

6. Dry at 125°F for 4 to 8 hours until the chips are crispy and the centers are done.

KALE CHIPS

*Flavor kale chips with your favorite seasoning blend, or eat them "naked."
Consider these blends: lemon pepper, salt and pepper (simple but very tasty,
especially tossed with apple cider vinegar), or Cajun seasoning blend.*

Yield: 2 cups **Prep time:** 5 minutes **Cook time:** 4 to 6 hours

1 bunch kale, stems removed

1 tablespoon olive oil or apple cider vinegar

seasoning, as desired

1. Cut the kale leaves into 2- to 3-inch strips.

2. Brush the kale lightly with olive oil or use apple cider vinegar as a low-fat alternative to oil. This gives the seasoning something to adhere to.

3. Sprinkle the kale with your choice of seasoning.

4. Lay the seasoned kale onto dehydrator trays and dry at 125°F for 4 to 6 hours, until they are crisp.

ZUCCHINI CHIPS

The spice measurements below are just suggestions. Start with these spice measurements; you'll know how to adjust to your taste after the first batch. Use 1 teaspoon chili powder for mild, 2 teaspoons for medium, and 3 teaspoons for a spicy chip.

Yield: 5 cups   **Prep time:** 15 minutes   **Cook time:** 10 to 12 hours

4 medium zucchini squash

¼ cup apple cider vinegar

salt, to taste

pepper, to taste

chili powder, to taste

1. Slice the zucchini into ¼-inch-thick rounds. It's best to keep the thickness the same for even drying. Experiment with using a crinkle cut slicing blade that makes ridges in the chips; the ridges tend to give spices more area to grab onto.

2. Add apple cider vinegar, salt, pepper, and chili powder to a wide bottomed, nonreactive bowl. Stir until incorporated.

3. Add a handful of raw chips to the bowl and toss until they are just coated with the vinegar and spice mix. Separate any pieces that stick together and make sure that all the zucchini slices are coated with the spices.

4. Arrange the chips on dehydrator trays. They can touch but should not overlap.

5. Dry at 135°F for 10 to 12 hours. If you have a bottom-heating dehydrator, you may need to rearrange the trays halfway through the drying cycle. After 5 hours, move the top trays to the bottom so the chips will be evenly dried.

CAJUN SEASONING BLEND

This is a versatile blend that we use when making kale or zucchini chips. We also add it to soup and skillet meals. Store seasoning blends in an airtight container in the pantry, for up to a year.

Yield: 1½ cups

¼ cup garlic powder

¼ cup kosher or sea salt

½ cup paprika

2 tablespoons pepper

2 tablespoons onion powder

2 tablespoons dried oregano

1 tablespoon dried thyme

1 tablespoon cayenne powder (optional)

Mix all the ingredients into a jar with enough room to shake the ingredients.

DEHYDRATED REFRIGERATOR PICKLES

Many other dehydrated vegetables can be pickled following this method, such as green beans, okra, zucchini, carrots, garlic scrapes, etc. Swap out the dill seed for turmeric, black peppercorns, or mustard seeds. Pick your favorite vinegar: apple cider, white, balsamic, or red or white wine. Experiment to find your family's favorite recipe.

Yield: 1 pint   **Prep time:** 5 minutes   **Cook time:** At least 24-hour wait time

1 cup vinegar

1 cup water

1½ tablespoons pickling salt or kosher salt

1 garlic clove, smashed

¼ teaspoon dill seed

⅛ teaspoon red pepper flakes

1½ cups dehydrated cucumber slices or spears

1. To prepare the brine, combine vinegar, water, and salt in a small saucepan over high heat. Bring to a rolling boil, then remove immediately and allow to cool.

2. Add the garlic, dill seed, red pepper flakes, and dehydrated cucumber slices to a pint-size canning jar.

3. Pour the cooled brine over the cucumbers, filling the jar to within ½ inch of the top. You might not use all the brine.

4. Refrigerate for at least 24 hours before eating. The cucumbers will plump and magically become pickles overnight.

MY CLASSIC BEEF JERKY

Use a lean cut of beef, like eye round roast, top round roast, or bottom round roast.

Yield: ¾ pound **Prep time:** 15 minutes, plus overnight
Cook time: 5 to 8 hours

1½ pounds lean beef

2 cups white vinegar

Classic Beef Brine

¼ cup soy sauce

⅓ cup Worcestershire sauce

1 tablespoon barbecue sauce

½ teaspoon pepper

½ teaspoon salt

½ teaspoon onion

½ teaspoon garlic

1. Cut beef into ¼-inch slices.

2. In a medium bowl, pretreat the beef slices with the white vinegar for 10 minutes. Drain and discard the white vinegar.

3. Add the drained beef slices and brine ingredients to a 1-gallon zip-top bag. Add water, if necessary, to completely cover the meat. Soak overnight in the refrigerator.

4. The next day, drain the brine, lay out the meat so the pieces do not touch, and dehydrate at 160°F for 5 to 8 hours until crisp but pliable.

Teriyaki Brine: For an Asian twist, use these ingredients for the brine: ⅔ cup teriyaki sauce, 1 tablespoon soy sauce, ½ cup water or pineapple juice, ½ teaspoon onion powder, ½ teaspoon fresh garlic , ½ teaspoon salt, and ½ teaspoon pepper.

Spicy Cajun Brine: If you like spicy, try a Cajun brine: ½ cup balsamic vinegar, ⅓ cup Worcestershire sauce, ⅓ cup water, 1 tablespoon molasses, 1 tablespoon Cajun spice, 1 teaspoon smoked paprika, ½ teaspoon salt, ½ teaspoon pepper, and ¼ teaspoon cayenne powder.

BEEF STEAK JERKY

Use a lean cut of beef, like eye round roast, top round roast, or bottom round roast.

Yield: ¾ pound   **Prep time:** 15 minutes, plus overnight
Cook time: 5 to 8 hours

1½ pounds lean beef

2 cups white vinegar

Beef Steak Brine

¼ cup balsamic vinegar

⅓ cup Worcestershire sauce

1 tablespoon molasses

1 tablespoon Steak Seasoning Blend (see recipe below)

1 teaspoon fresh garlic

1 teaspoon onion powder

1. Cut beef into ¼-inch slices.

2. In a medium bowl, pretreat the beef slices with the white vinegar for 10 minutes. Drain and discard the white vinegar.

3. Add the drained beef slices and brine ingredients to a 1-gallon zip-top bag. Add water, if necessary, to completely cover the meat. Soak overnight in the refrigerator.

4. The next day, drain the brine, lay out the meat so the pieces do not touch, and dehydrate at 160°F for 5 to 8 hours until crisp but pliable.

STEAK SEASONING BLEND

2 tablespoons coarse salt

1 tablespoon pepper

1 tablespoon coriander

1 tablespoon mustard seed

½ tablespoon dill seed

½ tablespoon red pepper flakes

Mix together and run through a spice mill or coffee grinder to get a powder. Use ½ tablespoon per 1½ pounds of meat.

CAULIFLOWER SOUP

Make this soup your own by adding your choice of seasonings: cumin, parsley, and basil all work well. Serve with an added pinch of cheese for garnish.

Yield: 6 cups   **Prep time:** 40 minutes   **Cook time:** 15 minutes

2 cups dehydrated cauliflower

⅛ cup dehydrated onion

⅛ cup dehydrated celery

2 slices dehydrated garlic

2½ cups water

⅛ cup quinoa

4 cups vegetable stock

pepper, to taste

salt, to taste

seasoning, to taste

1. Place cauliflower, onion, celery, and garlic in a large bowl and cover with 2½ cups boiling water. Soak until vegetables are almost rehydrated, about 30 minutes. Drain and discard soaking liquid.

2. In a large saucepan, add the vegetables, quinoa, vegetable stock, salt, pepper, and seasoning, to taste. Cook over medium heat for 15 minutes, until the cauliflower and quinoa are soft and fully cooked.

3. Remove from heat and pour small batches into a blender to mix. Be careful—it will be very hot. Blend until smooth, 45 to 60 seconds.

ASPARAGUS SOUP

Yield: 6 cups   **Prep time:** 10 minutes   **Cook time:** 20 minutes

2 cups dehydrated asparagus

1 cup water

2 tablespoons butter or extra virgin olive oil

½ teaspoon dried basil or 10 fresh basil leaves, chopped

4 cups chicken broth or stock

salt and pepper, to taste

1. Place the asparagus and water in a saucepan and simmer over medium heat for 5 to 10 minutes until the asparagus pieces are plump. Drain and reserve asparagus liquid.

2. Add the asparagus, butter, and basil to a stockpot at medium heat until the butter is melted, about 1 minute.

3. Add the chicken stock and asparagus water to the stockpot and bring heat up to high until the mixture comes to a boil.

Reduce heat and simmer for 10 minutes. Remove from heat and cool about 5 minutes.

4. In small batches, pour the warm soup into a blender and puree to desired texture. After pureeing, transfer small batches to a large bowl to keep them separate. I like to keep a few blender batches with larger pieces, so the soup has texture.

5. Return mixture to the stockpot and add salt and pepper to taste.

THERMOS VEGETABLE SOUP

Your Thermos is handy for rehydrating food and also works well as a cooker. Make this in the morning, and it will be ready to eat by lunchtime. Combine any dried vegetables for this soup, including peas, tomatoes, broccoli, onion, zucchini, celery, and carrots. This works best if your vegetables are all approximately the same size.

Yield: 2 cups   **Prep time:** 5 minutes   **Cook time:** 4 hours

⅓ cup dried vegetables

¼ teaspoon dried parsley

¼ teaspoon dried sweet basil

pinch garlic powder

pinch onion powder

salt and pepper, to taste

1 tablespoon spaghetti, broken into small sections

2 cups boiling chicken or beef broth

1. Fill an empty Thermos with boiling water. Just before you pack the ingredients in the Thermos, pour out the hot water.

2. Add the dried vegetables, parsley, basil, garlic powder, onion powder, salt, pepper, and pasta to the Thermos.

3. Bring the chicken or beef broth to a rolling boil and pour over dry ingredients. Quickly cover the Thermos and close securely. If possible, shake or turn over the Thermos every hour until ready to eat.

SWEET POTATO COCONUT FLOUR PANCAKES

Yield: 6 medium pancakes   **Prep time:** 5 minutes
Cook time: 2 to 4 minutes

5 eggs

¼ cup milk

½ teaspoon vanilla extract

½ cup unsweetened applesauce

¼ cup coconut flour

¼ cup sweet potato flour

1 tablespoon granulated sugar or honey

¼ teaspoon baking powder

ground cinnamon, to taste

¼ teaspoon salt

1. Preheat a griddle or large skillet over medium heat.

2. In a large bowl, whisk eggs, milk, vanilla, and applesauce until combined.

3. In a medium bowl, whisk coconut flour, sweet potato flour, sugar or honey, baking powder, cinnamon, and salt until well blended.

4. Add dry ingredients to wet ingredients. Stir with a fork until ingredients are well combined and no lumps remain.

5. Drop batter by the ladleful, approximately ¼ cup at a time, onto the hot griddle. Cook 2 to 4 minutes per side until small bubbles begin to form on top, then flip.

6. Serve warm with your favorite pancake toppings.

SLOW COOKER STUFFED CABBAGE ROLLS

Yield: 8 to 12 rolls   **Prep time:** 20 minutes   **Cook time:** 8 to 10 hours

8 to 12 dehydrated cabbage leaves

¼ cup dehydrated diced onion

⅔ cup tomato powder

1 tablespoon brown sugar (optional)

1 teaspoon Worcestershire sauce (optional)

1 cup cooked white rice

1 egg, beaten

1 pound extra-lean ground beef

1 teaspoon salt, plus more to taste

1 teaspoon pepper, plus more to taste

1. Bring a large pot of water to a boil. Add dehydrated cabbage leaves and boil for 2 to 3 minutes, until soft. Drain and set aside.

2. In a small bowl, cover diced onion with hot water to rehydrate, about 15 minutes.

3. To make tomato sauce, put the tomato powder in a medium bowl. Slowly pour in 2 cups of boiling water and whisk well to reduce chunks. Whisk in brown sugar and Worcestershire sauce, if using. Set aside.

4. In a large bowl, combine cooked rice, egg, ground beef, onion, 2 tablespoons tomato sauce, salt, and pepper. Stir with a spoon, or dig in and mush with clean hands.

5. Place about ¼ cup of the mixture in each cabbage leaf, roll up, and tuck ends in. Place rolls in slow cooker.

6. Pour remaining tomato sauce over cabbage rolls. Cover and cook on low 8 to 10 hours.

SAUTÉED WINTER SQUASH WITH APPLES

Yield: 2 cups   **Prep time:** 1 hour   **Cook time:** 10 minutes

1 cup dehydrated winter squash cubes

½ cup dehydrated onion

½ cup dehydrated apple

2 tablespoons butter

½ teaspoon celery salt

½ teaspoon garlic powder

½ teaspoon thyme

salt, to taste

pepper, to taste

1. Place dehydrated squash cubes and onion in a large bowl and cover with 2 cups of warm water. Soak for 1 hour. Drain any remaining water.

2. Rehydrate the apple by placing it in a separate bowl and covering with cool water for 1 hour.

3. Melt the butter in a large saucepan over medium heat.

4. Add the squash, onion, and celery salt to the saucepan, stirring occasionally until the squash begins to brown, about 5 minutes.

5. Add the garlic powder and apple, cooking until the apples are tender, about 2 minutes.

6. Add thyme, salt, and pepper to taste.

DEHYDRATED WINTER SQUASH NESTS

These squash nests will be cooked before eating, so it is not necessary to blanch them. However, you may find that peeling and spiralizing is easier if the squash has been cooked in a microwave for 3 minutes after seeding. Delicata and butternut squash work well for this recipe.

Yield: 10 to 15 squash nests   **Prep time:** 30 minutes   **Cook time:** 4 to 6 hours

1 large winter squash, peeled and deseeded

1. If using a spiralizer, cut the squash into manageable pieces and shred the squash into long strands. If you don't have a spiralizer, draw a vegetable peeler down over the squash, making thin, broad, noodle-like slices, or use a julienne peeler to get spaghetti-like strands.

2. Not all the pieces will spiral in one long section, so separate the parts that do by removing them from the pile.

3. Add the long strands to dehydrator trays and arrange them in a nest by piling each piece on top of itself. Add the smaller pieces to dehydrator trays in small handfuls to form nests, 5 or 6 piles to a tray.

4. Dry at 140°F for 2 hours, turn heat down to 130°F and dry an additional 2 to 4 hours until the pieces are brittle.

GARLIC CREOLE SPICED SQUASH NESTS

Yield: 10 nests   **Prep time:** 35 minutes   **Cook time:** 5 minutes

10 Dehydrated Winter Squash Nests (page 157), or 2 cups dried squash shreds

⅓ cup all-purpose flour

2 cloves garlic, minced

2 large eggs, beaten

1 tablespoon Creole Spice Blend

2 tablespoons olive oil

10 teaspoons cheddar cheese

1. Partially rehydrate the squash nests by soaking in hot water for 30 minutes. Drain and discard soaking liquid.

2. In a large bowl, combine flour, garlic, eggs, and Creole seasoning. Dip the butternut squash nests in the egg mixture, taking care not to break apart the nests.

3. Heat olive oil in a large skillet over medium-high heat.

4. Scoop out 1 nest for each serving. Place in the skillet and flatten the squash with a spatula, then cook until the underside is golden brown, about 2 minutes.

5. Flip and cook on the other side, about 2 minutes longer.

6. Top each nest with 1 teaspoon of cheddar cheese and serve immediately.

CREOLE SPICE BLEND

Yield: about ½ cup

1 tablespoon onion powder

1 tablespoon garlic powder

1 tablespoon dried basil

½ tablespoon dried thyme

½ tablespoon black pepper

½ tablespoon white pepper

½ tablespoon cayenne pepper

2½ tablespoons paprika

1½ tablespoons salt

Combine onion powder, garlic powder, dried basil, dried thyme, pepper, paprika, and salt in a small bowl. Mix thoroughly.

FAJITA BEANS AND RICE

This is a spicy blend; omit cayenne pepper for a mild version.

Yield: 1 pint jar dry; 6 cups cooked   **Prep time:** 35 minutes
Cook time: 20 to 25 minutes

1 cup Quick Brown Rice (page 163)

2 cups Quick Cook Beans (page 164)

¼ cup dehydrated sweet bell pepper

¼ cup dehydrated onion

¼ cup dehydrated carrot

¼ cup tomato powder

¼ teaspoon dried garlic

1 teaspoon chili powder

½ teaspoon salt

½ teaspoon paprika

½ teaspoon brown sugar

¼ teaspoon black pepper

¼ teaspoon oregano

¼ teaspoon cumin

⅛ teaspoon cayenne pepper

1. Place all ingredients in a 1-pint wide-mouth jar or Mylar bag. Add a 100cc oxygen absorber and seal tightly. Store for up to 5 years.

2. To serve, remove the oxygen packet and empty the contents of the jar into a large skillet. Cover with 6 cups water and bring to a boil over high heat. Reduce heat to medium, cover, and simmer for 15 to 20 minutes, occasionally stirring until the beans are done.

3. Garnish with grated cheese, to taste.

RICED CAULIFLOWER PIZZA CRUST

This cauliflower crust is a healthy alternative to traditional pizza crusts. Substitute one quarter of the cheese with a low-fat alternative to reduce calories.

Yield: 2 (8-inch) crusts **Prep time:** 40 minutes
Cook time: 15 to 20 minutes

1 cup dehydrated cauliflower

4 cups water

2 eggs

2 cups grated Parmesan cheese

1. Preheat oven to 400°F.

2. Place cauliflower in a large bowl, cover with 4 cups hot water, and soak for 20 minutes. Drain and discard soaking liquid.

3. Chop the rehydrated cauliflower by hand, or with a food processor, until the pieces are small and uniform in size.

4. Cook the riced cauliflower in a skillet over medium heat. Stir until cauliflower is dry and the moisture is removed.

5. Set the cauliflower aside and allow it to cool. It may cool faster if it is removed from the skillet.

6. In a separate bowl, whisk the eggs. Mix in Parmesan cheese.

7. Add cooled cauliflower to the bowl, and stir until completely mixed.

8. Working on parchment paper, split the mixture into 2 equal portions. Work each piece into an 8-inch circle, about ¼ inch thick. Keep more of the mixture on the edges so the rounds will cook evenly and the edges will not burn.

9. Slide the parchment paper onto a baking sheet and cook at 400°F until the rounds are browned and firm, about 15 to 20 minutes.

Ideas for Serving Cauliflower Crust

• *Spread with tomato sauce, spices, cheese, and pizza toppings. Bake like a pizza for 10 to 15 minutes until the cheese melts and the toppings are cooked.*

• *Spread with tomato sauce, spices, and toppings. Roll into a log and bake on parchment paper for 15 minutes. Top with cheese, green onions, and sour cream. Cut into 1-inch sections to serve.*

• *After the crust has cooled, section the crust into 16 equal strips. Sprinkle with your favorite spices (see Cajun Seasoning Blend on page 147), then reheat at 400°F for 10 minutes. The strips will be a tasty, crisp snack.*

HASH BROWN MIX IN A JAR

Dry the ingredients separately and combine. This recipe makes 1 jar, with 2 meals.

Yield: 1 pint jar dry; 2 cups cooked **Prep time:** 10 to 15 minutes
Cook time: 10 to 15 minutes

2 cups dehydrated potato shreds

½ cup dried onion

½ cup dried sweet pepper

¼ cup dried minced garlic

1 teaspoon vegetable oil

1. Mix the potato shreds, dried onion, dried sweet pepper, and dried minced garlic in a large bowl. Place in a canning jar or Mylar bag. Add a 100cc oxygen absorber and seal tightly. Store for up to 5 years.

2. To prepare, empty 1 cup of the jar's contents into a bowl and cover with boiling water for 10 to 15 minutes until plump. Strain and squeeze to remove excess water.

3. Heat oil in a skillet over medium heat.

4. Add potato mixture to the skillet, gently pressing into a thin, even layer as it cooks.

5. Cook until very crispy and brown each side for approximately 3 minutes.

QUICK BROWN RICE

Store dehydrated rice in canning jars with 100cc oxygen absorbers, or remove oxygen with a FoodSaver attachment. Due to the high fat content of brown rice, Quick Brown Rice should be used within 6 months.

Yield: 2 cups dehydrated rice; 3½ cups cooked rice
Prep time: 5 to 7 hours   **Cook time:** 17 minutes

1. Cook 2 cups of regular brown rice according to package directions; make sure all liquid is absorbed.

2. Cover your dehydrator trays with parchment paper or Paraflexx liners and spread the cooked rice in a single layer. Dehydrate at 125°F for 5 to 7 hours. Midway through the drying process, break up any rice that is stuck together and rotate trays. When fully dry, the rice should click when dropped on a tabletop.

3. To rehydrate, measure 1 cup of dried rice, place in a saucepan, and cover with ¾ cup water. Soak for 5 minutes to begin rehydration, then bring to boil and boil for 2 minutes. Remove from heat, cover, and let sit 10 minutes. Fluff with a fork.

QUICK COOK BEANS

Yield: 3 cups   **Prep time:** 10 minutes, plus 8 hours   **Cook time:** 8 to 10 hours

4 cups dry beans

1. Soak dried beans overnight. Discard water.

2. After at least 8 hours of soaking, add the beans to a large pot, cover with water, and bring to a boil. Reduce heat and simmer for 10 minutes. Drain.

3. Spread the partially cooked beans in a single layer on dehydrator trays and process between 95°F and 100°F for 8 to 10 hours. They will be hard when dry.

4. Store in canning jars with 100cc oxygen absorbers or remove oxygen with a FoodSaver attachment. The shelf life is 5 years.

To rehydrate: Soak 1 cup dehydrated beans and 2 cups water in a saucepan for 5 minutes. Bring to a rolling boil for 10 minutes. Do not cover.

MRS. B'S STOVETOP BAKED BEANS

Yield: 3 cups   **Prep time:** 15 minutes   **Cook time:** 10 minutes

1 cup Quick Cook Beans (page 164)

2 cups water

¼ cup dehydrated chopped onion

2 teaspoons mustard

⅛ cup packed brown sugar, or to taste

1 teaspoon Worcestershire sauce

1. Rehydrate the Quick Cook Beans by soaking the beans with 2 cups water in a saucepan for 5 minutes. Bring to a rolling boil for 10 minutes. Do not cover.

2. Add the remaining ingredients. Stir until brown sugar is dissolved.

3. Reduce the heat to medium and simmer for an additional 5 minutes until beans are soft and sauce forms. Add additional water in 1-teaspoon increments, if needed.

MEXICAN FIESTA BAKE

Yield: 1 (2½-quart) baking dish   **Prep time:** 45 minutes
Cook time: 15 minutes

1 cup dehydrated tomatoes

1 cup fresh or dehydrated cilantro leaves

½ cup dehydrated, diced green pepper

½ cup dehydrated corn kernels

¼ cup tomato powder

2 fresh jalapeño peppers

2 cups ground beef

1 teaspoon garlic

1 lime, juiced

6 corn tortillas, cut into 1-inch squares

1 cup cheddar cheese

1. Preheat oven to 350°F.

2. Place the dehydrated tomatoes in a small bowl and cover with 2 cups of cool water for 30 minutes, or until plump and tender. Drain and dice into bite-sized pieces.

3. Place the cilantro leaves, diced green pepper, and corn in a small bowl and add enough cool water to cover. Let soak for 10 to 15 minutes or until peppers plump. Drain.

4. To make tomato sauce, slowly add 12 ounces of hot water to

¼ cup tomato powder. Mix until smooth. Set aside.

5. Clean, seed, and dice 2 fresh jalapeño peppers.

6. Cook the ground beef in a large skillet until completely browned.

7. Add the tomato sauce, garlic, lime juice, tomato, cilantro, green pepper, corn, tortillas, and jalapeño to the ground beef. Stir, and heat throughout.

8. Transfer to a 2½-quart baking dish and top with cheese.

9. Bake for 15 minutes until the cheese is bubbly.

ROSE HIP MINT TEA

Rose hips have more vitamin C than most citrus fruits. They are sweet and could be used on their own to make a tea, but the addition of mint makes this drink even more refreshing. This recipe is also a great help with stomach ailments and flatulence.

Don't throw out the rose hips once they've been used to make tea. Eat them, instead. They retain their nutritional value, so after you're done drinking the tea, add the rose hips to soups or serve them as a side at the supper table.

Yield: 1 cup　**Prep time:** 0 minutes　**Steep time:** 10 to 15 minutes

1 teaspoon dried rose hips

1 teaspoon dried spearmint or peppermint

1 cup water

1. Add the mint and rose hips to a French press or teapot and pour in 1 cup of hot water. Some tea makers grind their rose hips before using them, but it really is not necessary.

2. Cover and steep for 10 to 15 minutes. The longer you steep, the deeper the flavor and color will be.

ORANGE MINT TEA BLEND

Yield: 1 cup   **Prep time:** 5 minutes, plus rest time   **Steep time:** 10 minutes

2 tablespoons dried, chopped mint

2 tablespoons dried orange

3 or 4 whole cloves (optional)

1. Measure the dry ingredients into a coffee grinder or mortar and pestle and process until they are mixed into uniform pieces. Place in a jar with a tight lid and allow the flavor to develop for a few days.

2. Add 1 teaspoon of Orange Mint Tea Blend to a tea ball infuser, teapot, or French press. Cover and steep for 10 minutes. This also makes a refreshing iced tea.

LEMON VERBENA SUN TEA

Lemon verbena is medicinally known as a digestive herb. It helps soothe indigestion, flatulence, and colic. It is mildly astringent, and using it to create a rinse for your mouth can help ward off candida.

Yield: 1 quart   **Prep time:** 0 minutes   **Steep time:** several hours

1 handful dried lemon verbena leaves

1 quart water

1. Crush a handful of dried leaves and add them to a large glass jar.

2. Cover leaves with 1 quart water and let the jar sit out in the sun for several hours.

3. Strain the leaves and add ice to enjoy a refreshing drink.

LEMONADE WITH DEHYDRATED CITRUS

Yield: 5 quarts   **Prep time:** 0 minutes   **Cook time:** 3 hours rest time

1 cup sugar

5 quarts water

15 pieces dehydrated citrus rounds

1. Add the sugar to 5 quarts water and stir until dissolved.

2. Add citrus pieces and stir.

3. Add ice to help keep the rinds submerged. Let it sit for at least 3 hours.

4. Stir and pour into glasses with some of the rehydrated citrus rounds as a garnish.

APPLE CRISP WITH OAT TOPPING

Yield: 1 (8 x 8-inch) glass pan   **Prep time:** 35 minutes
Cook time: 30 minutes

3 cups dehydrated apple slices

¾ cup sugar, divided

2 tablespoons cornstarch

½ cup flour

½ cup oats

pinch salt

⅛ teaspoon ground cinnamon, plus more, to taste

½ stick cold butter

1. Preheat oven to 375° F. Prepare an 8 x 8-inch glass pan with cooking spray.

2. Place the apple slices in a bowl and add just enough hot water to cover. Let it sit for 30 minutes. Drain and reserve the liquid.

3. Toss the rehydrated apples with ½ cup sugar and cinnamon, to taste.

4. In a measuring cup, mix cornstarch and 2 tablespoons cold water until completely incorporated and no lumps remain.

5. Place the apples and reserved liquid into a medium saucepan and simmer for 5 minutes. Add the cornstarch slurry and heat until the mixture thickens. If the apples look too dry, add more liquid, 1 tablespoon at a time,

until you reach the consistency you want.

6. Spoon the apples into the prepared pan, pushing down, so the apples are covered in the sauce.

7. To create the topping, add the flour, oats, remaining sugar, salt, and ⅛ teaspoon cinnamon to a small bowl. Using a pastry blender or food processor, cut the cold butter into the dry ingredients until the mixture resembles coarse crumbs.

8. Pour the topping over the apple filling and spread evenly until it reaches all corners. Bake for 30 minutes until the topping is golden brown and the filling is bubbling.

STEVE'S LOW-FAT PINEAPPLE CAKE

This recipe is a family favorite that has been adapted for low-fat diets. It is not overly sweet, but it satisfies your cravings.

Yield: 1 (8 x 8-inch) cake **Prep time:** 25 minutes
Cook time: 25 to 30 minutes

4 cups dehydrated pineapple

2 cups water

2¼ cups all-purpose flour

1 cup granulated sugar

2 teaspoons baking soda

pinch salt

2 teaspoons vanilla extract

2 eggs

1 (3.5-ounce) package sugar-free vanilla instant pudding

1½ cups fat-free whipped cream

1. Preheat oven to 350° F. Grease and flour an 8 x 8-inch baking dish.

2. Crush the dehydrated pineapple in a plastic zip-top bag with a rolling pin, or pulse in a food processor. Pineapple should be in pieces, not powdered. Reserve 2 cups.

3. Put the rest of the crushed pineapple in a small bowl and completely cover with 2 cups cool tap water for 15 to 20 minutes. Add more water if needed. Drain and reserve the pineapple liquid.

4. In a medium bowl, whisk together the flour, sugar, baking soda, and salt.

5. Add the vanilla extract and eggs to the small bowl with rehydrated pineapple, and mix.

6. Add the wet ingredients to the dry and stir until batter forms.

7. Pour the batter into the prepared baking dish.

8. Bake for 25 to 30 minutes until the cake is golden brown and a toothpick comes out clean. Let cool before adding topping.

9. Whisk the 2 cups crushed pineapple, pineapple liquid, and sugar-free pudding mix together until combined. Add extra water in 1-teaspoon increments, if needed. Gently fold in the whipping cream until incorporated.

10. Spread topping over the cake. Refrigerate until ready to serve.

CANDIED GINGER

You can save and store the ginger syrup from step 5 in your refrigerator for up to 2 months. If you find that you've run out of syrup, you can use the candied ginger to make more.

Yield: 8 ounces candied ginger   **Prep time:** 40 minutes, plus 1 hour conditioning time   **Cook time:** 4 to 6 hours

1 large (8-ounce) ginger root

4 cups water

2¼ cups sugar, divided

1. Wash and peel the ginger root. Using a mandoline, cut the root into ⅛-inch slices.

2. Add 4 cups water and 2 cups sugar to the saucepan, and stir until sugar is dissolved.

3. Add the ginger pieces to the saucepan, and bring to a boil.

4. Reduce the heat to a simmer and cook for 30 minutes, keeping the saucepan partially uncovered so steam can escape.

5. Strain the ginger mixture and save the syrup in a canning jar.

6. Place the ginger pieces on a rack or dehydrating tray for one hour to condition, until they are sticky but not wet.

7. Toss the pieces in the remaining ¼ cup sugar until they are lightly coated. You can skip this part and cut down on the sugar content; they will still taste sweet from the simple syrup.

8. Place ginger slices on the dehydrator tray and dry at 135°F for 4 to 6 hours or until the pieces are pliable but not sticky inside.

You can create a ginger syrup 3 times, with the same ginger root, without changing the taste of the ginger. Once you save the syrup, return the ginger root to the pan, add another 4 cups water and 2 cups sugar and simmer for another 30 minutes.

Here are 5 ways you can use ginger simple syrup:

1. Add to warm tea in place of sweetener

2. Pour over pancakes or waffles

3. Top your ice cream

4. Use in salad dressing

5. Bake with winter squash

OATMEAL FIG COOKIES

Fig and oatmeal just naturally go together. Use your favorite recipe and add fruit or use this timeless classic.

Yield: 2 dozen cookies   **Prep time:** 10 minutes, plus 1 hour chill time
Cook time: 12 to 14 minutes

1½ cups all-purpose flour

1 teaspoon baking powder

½ teaspoon salt

3 cups old-fashioned rolled oats (for a softer cookie, process half the oats in a blender until finely ground)

1 cup butter, softened to room temperature

1 cup packed brown sugar

½ cup granulated sugar

2 eggs

1 teaspoon vanilla extract

1 cup rehydrated figs, cut into pieces

1. Preheat oven to 350° F. Line baking sheets with parchment paper.

2. In a large bowl, whisk the flour, baking powder, and salt. Stir in the oats.

3. In another large bowl, cream the butter and sugars with a hand mixer. Add the eggs and vanilla, then cream again.

4. Add the flour mixture to the liquid, then stir until combined. Stir in the rehydrated fig pieces.

5. Chill the dough for 1 hour or overnight.

6. Place tablespoon-sized scoops onto the baking sheets, spacing cookies 2 inches apart. Bake for 12 to 14 minutes, until cookies are lightly browned.

CONVERSIONS

Common Conversions

1 gallon = 4 quarts = 8 pints = 16 cups = 128 fluid ounces = 3.8 liters

1 quart = 2 pints = 4 cups = 32 ounces = .95 liter

1 pint = 2 cups = 16 ounces = 480 ml

1 cup = 8 ounces = 240 ml

¼ cup = 4 tablespoons = 12 teaspoons = 2 ounces = 60 ml

1 tablespoon = 3 teaspoons = ½ fluid ounce = 15 ml

Volume Conversions

US	US equivalent	Metric
1 tablespoon (3 teaspoons)	½ fluid ounce	15 milliliters
¼ cup	2 fluid ounces	60 milliliters
⅓ cup	3 fluid ounces	90 milliliters
½ cup	4 fluid ounces	120 milliliters
⅔ cup	5 fluid ounces	150 milliliters
¾ cup	6 fluid ounces	180 milliliters
1 cup	8 fluid ounces	240 milliliters
2 cups	16 fluid ounces	480 milliliters

Weight Conversions

US	Metric
½ ounce	15 grams
1 ounce	30 grams
2 ounces	60 grams
¼ pound	115 grams
⅓ pound	150 grams
½ pound	225 grams
¾ pound	350 grams
1 pound	450 grams

Temperature Conversions

Fahrenheit (°F)	Celsius (°C)
100°F	38°C
110°F	43°C
125°F	52°C
130°F	55°C
135°F	57°C
140°F	60°C
150°F	65°C
250°F	120°C
275°F	135°C
300°F	150°C
325°F	160°C
350°F	175°C
375°F	190°C
400°F	200°C

ACKNOWLEDGMENTS

A number of people made the writing of this book an easier, and more pleasant, task than it would otherwise have been. Casie Vogel and Shayna Keyles at Ulysses Press helped launch the project and held my hand every step of the way. I am grateful for their superior editing powers and the trust they have placed in this enthusiastic blogger looking to share her love of food preservation.

My husband Steve has also been with me every step, clearing the deck of other distractions so I could focus on the task at hand. Thanks for believing in me and for supporting the crazy projects that have been a part of our home for the past year. You are the best, my dear.

And finally, thanks to the Super Awesome Ladies. You truly are a terrific sounding board and cheering section.

ABOUT THE AUTHOR

Shelle Wells is the founder of the popular websites PreparednessMama .com, Rootsy.org, and RockinWHomestead.com, and believes that everyone should be prepared for the big and small disasters of life. She helps people do this by teaching them to build their food storage, grow a family garden, and be as self-reliant as possible no matter where they live.

Her brand of preparedness teaches practical self-reliance, not zombie apocalypse, and while she calls herself a prepper, there is no doomsday involved. She has been researching topics on preparedness, food storage, and gardening for over 20 years. A native Oregonian, she's currently transplanted in Central Texas on an 11-acre homestead with her husband, Steve.